Modern Korean Artists

Modern Korean Artists

This book, mainly a compilation of articles published in *Koreana*
from 2000 to 2008, is the second volume of the *Selections from Koreana* series.
Articles may have been edited due to style or space considerations.

The opinions expressed by the authors do not necessarily represent those of the editors of
Koreana or the Korea Foundation.

Published by the Korea Foundation

The Korea Foundation
Seocho P.O. Box 227
Diplomatic Center Building
2558 Nambusunhwanno, Seocho-gu
Seoul 137-863, Korea
Tel: (82-2) 2151-6542
Fax: (82-2) 2151-6592
Homepage: www.kf.or.kr

Editor-in-chief: Lee Kyong-hee
Copy Editor: Teresita M. Reed
Design & Layout: Kim's Communication Associates (www.gegd.co.kr)

Printed in Korea

Price: US$50.00 (in Korea: 50,000 won)

ISBN: 978-89-86090-33-8 (03600)

Modern Korean Artists

Korea Foundation
한국국제교류재단

FOREWORD

The Korea Foundation is pleased to present "Modern Korean Artists," the second volume of our *Selections from Koreana* series, which is intended to promote cross-cultural understanding by providing readers abroad with an introduction of representative Korean artists and their artistic pursuits.

"Modern Korean Artists," a compilation of articles about modern artists from the quarterly magazine *Koreana* (2000-2008), offers an opportunity for readers to better understand and appreciate Korea's modern arts, related to a variety of genres, ranging from the fine arts to cinema.

In addition, for the convenience of readers, the articles have been grouped into five general categories: fine arts artists, stage performers, musicians, film-related figures, and architects. Although the entire spectrum of Korea's modern arts and artists cannot be fully dealt with in a single publication such as this, it does include a close-up look of several key figures who have contributed to advancement of the modern arts scene in Korea.

The Korea Foundation thus hopes that this volume will serve as a useful information resource for readers to reflect upon the achievements of Korea's modern artists and to enrich their cultural diversity with unique aspects of Korean culture and arts. Moreover, this volume seeks to contribute to cultural understanding among peoples from a variety of cultures and backgrounds.

In particular, the Foundation is grateful to the professionals who have allowed us to use their photo images in this publication, as well as the various individuals that have assisted in the successful completion of this notable endeavor, with their thoughtful assistance and diligent efforts.

Yim Sung-joon
President
The Korea Foundation

CONTENTS

Fine Artists

Stage Artists

Musicians

Architects

Film Artists

Fine Artists

Park Soo-keun
The Common People's Artist

1

Y ou don't have to be a nationalist to have addressed the question, at some time or other, "What do you think is Korean beauty?" What does it mean to be beautiful to Koreans? For this question, however, there is no definitive answer, no way of saying, "This is what it is."

But when someone asks me what Korean beauty is, one artist comes immediately to mind: Park Soo-keun (1914–1965), whose nom de plume, Miseok, means "beautiful stone." Though his name is always preceded by epithets such as "the national artist," "painter of the lives of ordinary people," or "our beloved painter," it is hard to pinpoint exactly what in his work makes it definitively Korean.

A people's idea of beauty, or sense of what is beautiful, matures slowly over a long period of time, ripening in the folds of their history and lives. Hence from the outset it is difficult and probably foolish to try to define it in a single word.

Park Soo-keun's work can be said to reflect the Korean people's inner thoughts about life and living. From his own original perspective, Park honestly depicted the lives of ordinary people at one of the most difficult periods in

50/50

2

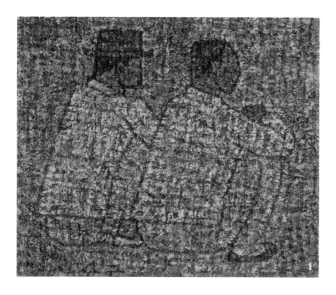

Korean history, the lives of the common people who held on despite the yoke of poverty and protected this land. He used a tough gritty matière, his perspective based on the Korean view of nature, to produce humble pictures of nature and people in grey tones with absolutely no decorativeness on surfaces resembling granite. He was the artist who captured with no pretensions the shared mentality of the Korean people and their outlook on nature. Park's art is about the most ordinary Korean people, living the kind of lives common to most Koreans.

With this in mind, what is the image we have of Park the artist? Do we really see him as an artist who captured our shared sensibilities as a people? Or are we blinded to who the artist really is by the dazzling prices his works fetch on the market? Sometimes I wonder if we find it hard to perceive the truth about the artist because of the famous name.

Such questions concerning Park stem from a lack of research about all modern Korean artists. Over the years we have turned a blind eye to the true nature of the artist, or saw his work in the light of his fame rather than taking an academic approach and discerning the real achievement and value of his art. Koreans do have a tendency to accept without question anything that is famous. Thus the

lack of research.

Compared to other artists, of course, the amount of research on Park is large, but studying his actual paintings has been difficult: much of the materials were lost during the period of Japanese colonial rule (1910–1945) and the Korean War (1950–1953), and the works that remained were scattered among private collectors and public institutions.

As a result Park's works have often been at the center of controversy. His early works, or experimental works that study the same subject from diverse angles — that is, works that depart from his typical style — have sometimes been declared as forgeries. Rather than understanding the artist's life as a whole and the flow and change of his art, the general approach has been to take certain works from a certain period as an absolute standard to judge all aspects of the artist. Park's style and typical subject matter were consistent from his early days. However, few paintings remain from his younger days in Yanggu, Chuncheon and Pyongyang. There are only illustrations in books and grainy photos from newspapers. Nevertheless, we make the mistake of reaching conclusions about his art based on a few impressionistic newspaper critiques and studies focusing on his paintings from the 1950s and 60s. Is this

From his own original perspective, Park honestly depicted the lives of ordinary people at one of the most difficult periods in Korean history, the lives of the common people who held on despite the yoke of poverty and protected this land.

the way we treat a "national artist?"

Park was born in Yanggu, Gangwon-do Province, which was part of North Korea before the Korean War. His parents were farmers and merchants, so his early life was affluent enough. But when he reached school age, his father's venture into a mining operation failed and the family entered tough times. Park's official résumé lists elementary school as his highest level of education. His teacher and school headmaster had noticed his talent for art, however, and provided him support that allowed him to continue his art while helping the family to make a living. In 1932, at the age of 18, he won a prize at the annual Joseon National Art Exhibition with a watercolor titled "Springtime Comes," and started his difficult career as an artist. In 1935 his ailing mother passed away and the family, thrown into even tougher circumstances, scattered all over the country. Park went alone to Chuncheon where he suffered all kinds of hardship. He continued to paint, however, and despite failing three years in a row at the national exhibition, he persevered and again won a prize in 1936.

In 1940 he married Kim Bok-sun, who was to be his partner and supporter all his life. He also got a job at the office of Pyongannam-do Province and started his married life in Pyongyang. Using his wife as a model, that year he painted "Woman Grinding Grain," which was accepted in the national exhibition. With his marriage he had gained a permanent model and his wife would often appear in later works.

As his daily life gained stability thanks to his job, he joined with other artists in the Pyongyang area such as Choi Yeong-rim, Chang Ri-seok and Hwang Yu-yeop to

1

1   "Oil Seller" (1960s)
    Woodblock print, 33 x 20.5 cm
2   "The Empty Cart" (1960s)
    Oil on hardboard, 21 x 30 cm

form an association named Juilhoe but when liberation from Japanese rule came in 1945 he moved to Geumseong, where he had already sent his family, and took a job as art teacher at Geumseong Middle School. He intended to focus on his art but then the Korean War broke out. Separating from his family, he came south on his own and worked as a wharf laborer in Gunsan. The work was tough but Park suffered most from the absence of his family. Spending his days grieving over the separation, in 1952 he was finally reunited with his wife and children when they came to the South as well.

Everyone who lived through that time was poor, but as refugees from the North, Park's family inevitably suffered grim poverty. He found a job, however, drawing portraits at the U.S. army base. Though by no means well off, by 1953 he had managed to save enough money to buy a

small house in Changsin-dong in Seoul, just outside Dongdaemun (East Gate). The next year, having gained some degree of financial stability, he quit his portrait painting job to concentrate on his own art.

For Park as the family breadwinner, art may have been something like a yoke whose shackles he wanted to escape. But he was fated to be tied to art all his life, and after his death art gave him the fame and honor that he never enjoyed while he was alive.

Despite his fame today, Park's career was fraught with difficulty. His early works were similar to those of any self-trained artist. They lacked technique and the composition was so unstable that they were characterized by naïveté. But from the first his subject was the everyday, such things as trees or women doing their work. Park steadily worked on these subjects and made them his own, and matching

1 "Dried Croakers" (1962)
  Oil on hardboard, 15.5 x 29 cm
2 "Three Women Selling Fruit" (Undated)
  Pencil on paper, 9.6 x 17.5 cm

with his own unique material he succeeded in creating works with a richly textured surface where the subject became one with the canvas.

In regard to his development as an artist, the start of his career can be identified as the early naïve days when he won a prize in 1932 at the national exhibition. From that time to 1952 he laid the foundations for his own style. In this period he first painted in watercolors and then did those same paintings in oil, creating the picture of resilient human nature that he had been seeking. At this time most of his paintings featured clear black outlines, as in a print, filled with grey tones.

The years from 1953, when he gained a steady job in the PX store at the U.S. army base and started painting in earnest to 1958, mark a period of self analysis and experimentation as Park forged his own style. In 1954 he quit his job to concentrate solely on painting. This was made possible by the support of several foreigners who had met Park at the base and understood his work: Mrs. Miller, Mrs. M. Henderson, Sylvia Zimmerman and John Ricks. In 1956 the Bando Art Gallery opened and Park's works, considered to exemplify Korean sentiment and aesthetics, began to sell like souvenirs.

The paintings from this time show thinner outlines and even a tendency toward meticulousness, and the surface of the painting begins to play a big role in Park's art. As a solid mass, the surface is not only very real; it is also the key to bringing out the composition of the picture plane. This is also the period when Park made his presence felt in the Korean art scene. In 1957, however, when a large painting that he had worked on so ambitiously failed to be accepted in the national exhibition, Park turned to drink in despair and began to ruin his health. The situation changed in 1959 when he was selected as a guest

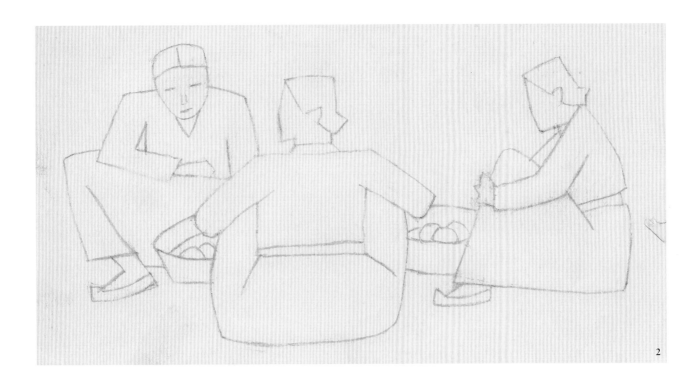

2

artist of the national exhibition and in 1962 he was asked to be a judge. The uneducated artist who had suffered all kinds of difficulties and ignominy finally found his place at the top of the art world. The style that we are familiar with and think of as typical Park Soo-keun was honed in the period from 1959 to the artist's death in 1965. He had developed and perfected his own style through ceaseless experimentation and repetition.

If the start of Park's career is seen as 1932, the year he first won a prize in the national exhibition, it took him 33 years to create his own style. In the end he spent only 12 years really concentrating on his art. From 1963, his work reaches the stage where the subject and the canvas are perfectly joined as one. The subject is fused into the canvas, the supporting background and the shapes of the subjects coming together as one entity that cannot be separated. Driven by passion, Park worked himself hard, abusing his health and his eyes for the sake of his art. The work was as tough as manual labor but such drive and passion made him the artist that we know today. Thus Park's distinctive flat, frontal style was created. The canvases that are like pieces of granite and the figures painted on them as if inscribed in stone are so fused together that there is no sense of distance.

Park's work shows us that his passion to create modern oil paintings that were definitively Korean were in complete unity with his life and ideals. Rather than being influenced by the fancy adjectives and language of speculative art theories, Park painted what he understood from his own life and thoughts, and the subjects in his surroundings. His sincerity as an artist provides much food for thought for the artists of today.

Jeong Jun-mo Art Critic / Culture Policy Adviser

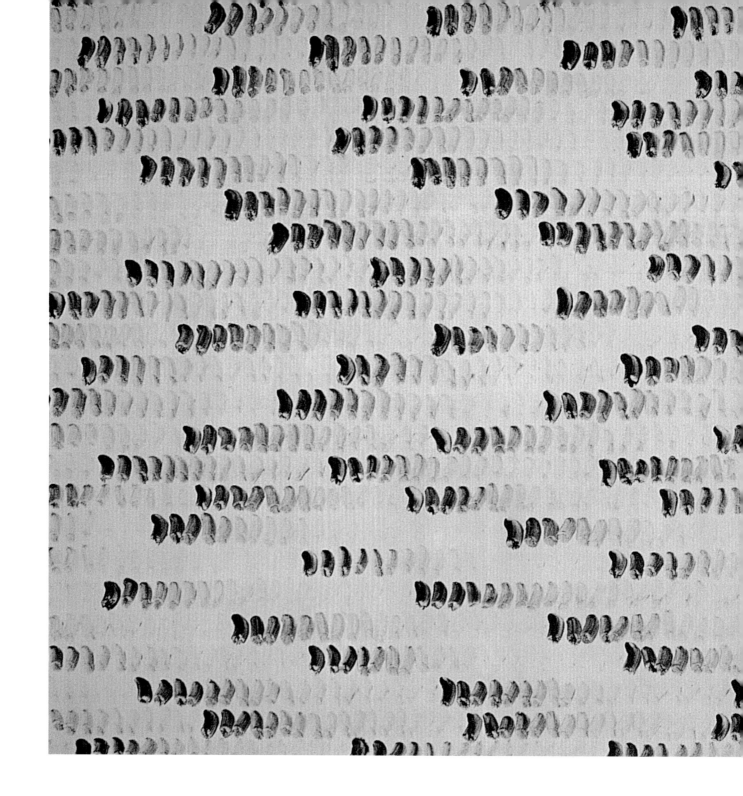

Lee U-fan

A Dot Opens Up an Infinite World

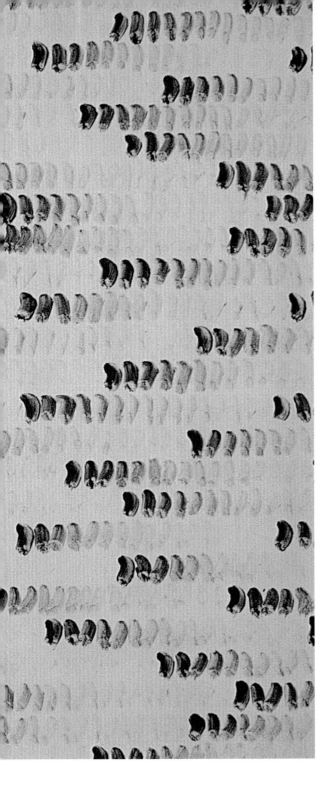

In the world of modern art, Korea is often represented by the painter Lee U-fan (Lee Ufan) and video/conceptual artist Paik Nam-june (Nam June Paik). Constantly crossing national and cultural boundaries at will, Lee calls himself a "wandering soul." Although he is a citizen of Korea and has spent the last 40 years in Japan, his work is more widely known in Europe.

However, a life of constant wandering can lead to a sense of unease. National biases and cultural differences produce misunderstandings and friction. Lee reflects that living on the edge of a precipice has given him a heightened artistic urge as well as intense tension. Even today, he keeps traveling back and forth between Korea, Japan and Europe, devoting all his energy to his work. Given the steady recognition he has received from leading art galleries overseas and the high praises bestowed on him by international critics, one may say that his name has already been written indelibly in the pages of art history.

Lee, born in 1936, has shown himself a man of many talents who lives life to the full. He was a major inspiration for Mono-ha, a leading avant-garde art movement in Japan, as well as the clear-thinking theorist who provided the movement with its philosophical foundation. His essay "From Object to Being," first presented in a 1969 competition, is a difficult text that applies profound philosophical principles to modern art; it is counted as one of the major critical studies that opened up a way for Japanese modern art to move forward. In 1970, Lee published a collection of critical pieces, *In Search of an Encounter*, which was fervently embraced by young Japanese artists while sparking off a "Lee Ufan fever" in Korea.

Lee has won recognition as a writer, not only for his critical essays, but also for more casual pieces that elaborate on random thoughts and insights gleaned from everyday life. Such gems as "Snake" and "The Acropolis and

"From Point" (1977)
Glue on canvas, 182 × 227cm

the Pebble," which appeared in another essay collection, *The Swift Current of Time*, have been included in Japanese high school textbooks. At the same time, he shows a deep love and knowledge of traditional Korean culture. His interest in folk paintings contributed greatly to the widespread research and rediscovery of Joseon period folk painting in the 1970s. The folk paintings he collected during that time were exhibited in France's Musée Guimet under the theme, "Nostalgie coréenne."

Born into a Confucian family in Haman, Gyeongsangnam-do Province, Lee studied poetry, calligraphy and painting from an early age. Although he had always favored literature over painting, he began to study Oriental painting at Seoul National University's College of Fine Arts. Before long, however, he stowed away on a ship to Japan, where he graduated from Nihon University as a philosophy major. A bookworm by nature, he read extensively in a wide variety of fields, including philosophy, culture and art. When he took up the life of a painter, he did so upon the foundation of the rich philosophical understanding and knowledge of art he had developed during the intervening years.

Lee soon shot to the forefront of modern art, constantly highlighting the most burning issues. His works could not be aligned with either Korean sentiment or Western rationality; they blended the two, offering a cogent critique of the aesthetic standards of both East and West, which intersected in his art.

"Relatum" (1986)
Iron and stone, 40 x 200 x 100 cm

The issue in modern painting is no longer what one paints, but what makes one an artist. Lee seeks the answer to this question not within his work itself, but in the relationship between his work and the outside world. His rejection of the idea of a work of art as a closed structure and his focus on its relationship with the outside world represents a breakthrough in modern art.

Because of their transcendental and contemplative ethos and their stress on the so-called blank space, Lee's works have been frequently equated with "Eastern mysticism." But Lee himself is critical of such views. He complains that the term "Eastern" is vague and unclear, its meaning changing with time, place and context. He is saddened when such a generalized term threatens to deprive him of his individuality.

Lee is skeptical of the artificial emphasis on national qualities in art. Tradition and national identity are not imbued artificially, but flow naturally from life within the work and from the world outside. Nation and tradition are not fixed entities formed long ago and handed down

unchanged ever since. Rather, they are open and flexible concepts, constantly redefined with the changing times.

In the foreword to *The Art of the Blank Space*, a book recently translated and published in Korea, Lee asks: "In this age when art is bankrupt, when humanity bows out, just how much novelty and necessity is there in expressing oneself with a few dots on a canvas or a few iron plates and rocks in a gallery?" In this question can be seen the artist's starting point and the intense speculation on modern art with which he has grappled.

The issue in modern painting is no longer what one paints, but what makes one an artist. Lee seeks the answer to this question not within his work itself, but in the rela-

1

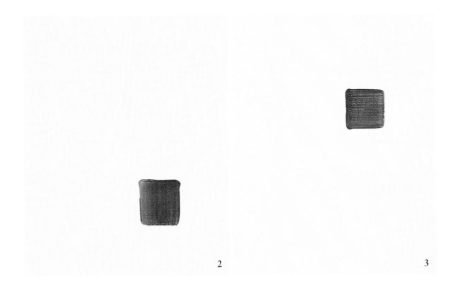

1 "Relatum" (1990)
   Iron and stone, 70 x 150 x 120 cm
2 "Correspondence" (1997)
   Glue on canvas, 92 x 73 cm
3 "Correspondence" (1997)
   Glue on canvas, 92 x 73 cm

2

3

tionship between his work and the outside world. His rejection of the idea of a work of art as a closed structure and his focus on its relationship with the outside world represents a breakthrough in modern art. He criticizes Western contemporary art for its total absorption in realizing the subjectivity of the artist. A work created solely by subjectivity leaves no room for a relationship with the outside world. For Lee, endless encounters with the world begin with his work, a passage connecting mind and matter, self and non-self, interior and exterior. This view of art has earned him the nickname "Artist of Encounter."

Consisting of diminishing dots, traces of rapid brushstrokes, or even an unframed canvas left completely blank except for a few small dots, Lee's paintings may seem puzzling to those unfamiliar with modern art. His sculptures are formed solely from heavy iron plates and stones either piled up or juxtaposed. However, it is these few dots or objects that hint at Lee's "endless encounters." If we focus only on the dots, we cannot see the world surrounding them. But if we open our eyes and minds to the blank space within which these dots are positioned, we can perceive a whole new world infinitely wider. The few

dots that Lee has drawn do not comprise "the painting"; they are merely the minimal marks required to make us perceive the blank space that is not drawn.

We might compare these isolated dots with a big drum. When the drum is struck, its sound resonates through the surrounding area. Ultimately, the space into which the sound spreads is the "blank space." The larger the blank space, the greater the resonance. Similarly, to appreciate Lee's works properly, you must open your mind and sense the blank space implied by the dots. Only then will you begin to feel the "outer frame" of the work and gain a new awareness of the space in which you are viewing the painting.

Seen and unseen, drawn and not drawn, empty and full — these opposites set up mutual relationships that open up limitless new worlds. This is what Lee means by the "aesthetics of encounter."

Through the blank space, he emphasizes the world of possibilities opening up through the "encounter," a vast panorama of relationships stretching out into infinity.

Lee Dong-seok Art Critic / Curator, Busan Metropolitan Art Museum

Park Seo-bo

Pioneer of Modern Abstract Painting

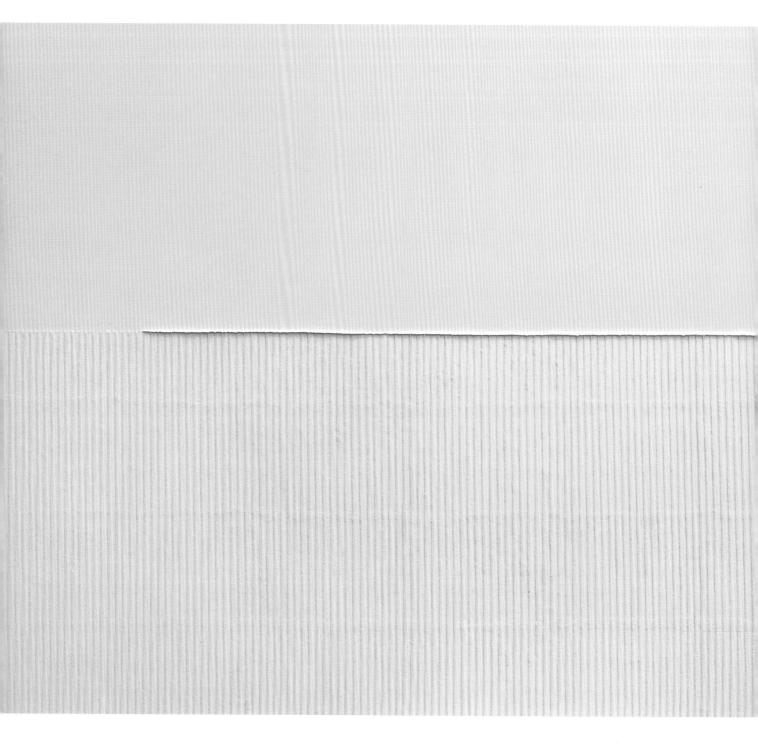

"Ecriture No. 071208" (2007)
Mixed media with Korean mulberry paper on canvas,
180 x 300 cm

The history of modern art in Korea is quite abbreviated. Korea's modern art got underway in earnest with the advent of abstract painting soon after the Korean War (1950–1953). Thereafter, Korea went on to achieve the rapid economic development that came to be known as the "Miracle of the Han," a result from the country's industrial advancement as well as its political and social stability. This dramatic transformation led to sweeping changes throughout society, including art and culture. In particular, modern art in Korea, after taking a cue from Western abstract art, declared independence from past tradition and developed rapidly.

The painter Park Seo-bo, born in 1931, emerged at this critical starting point of modern art. He played a leading role in the launch of a new era of post-war art by roiling the mainstream art circles with experimental creations, the likes of which had never been seen in Korea. The "Exhibition of Four Modern Artists" in 1956, which featured Park as the central figure, represented a public challenge to the established art world and the start of a new art movement. These brave artists distanced themselves from previous generations by rejecting state-sponsored exhibitions; they further shocked the public with their presentation of abstract paintings, dubbed "l'art informel," or the "non-conceptual art."

Park's l'art informel series, "Protoplasm," which was exhibited at this time, marked the beginning of abstract painting in Korea. Through his works, Park sought to have the public understand that painting was an abstraction that delved into the inner depths of humanity, into an intangible world beneath the surface. He recalls that "the formless, cell-dividing 'Protoplasm' symbolized pain, freedom and creative energy, through a new style of painting, which had no precedent in Korean art history."

From a technical perspective, his early works were

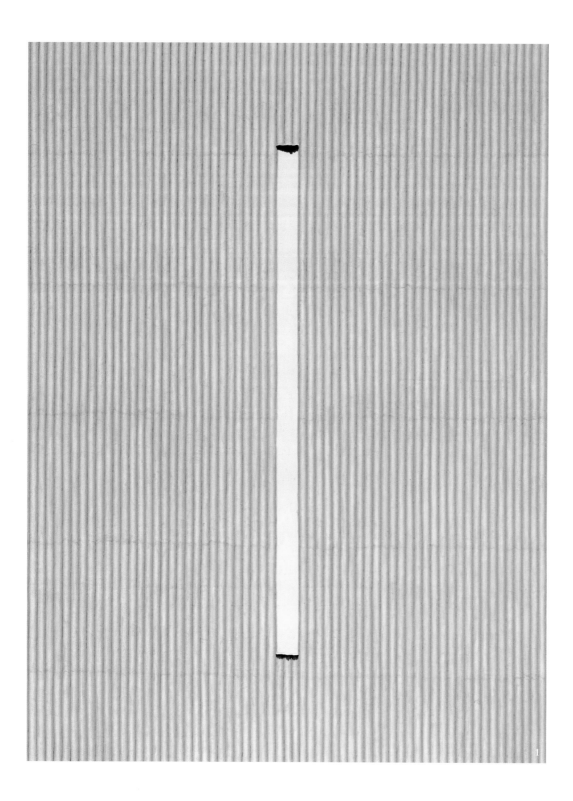

"Art is no longer a task of filling something but a task of emptying something, and thus must involve throwing yourself away. Art must no longer reign over people, it must comfort people."

heavily influenced by French l'art informel and American abstract expressionism. Park later began to explore the underlying essence of things rather than their physical appearance, leading to his departure from Western expressionism and a preference for achromatic colors and matière effects. His "Protoplasm" series, which above all expressed his personal experiences, is an artistic interpretation of the Korean conflict and the subsequent upheaval. With dark and somber achromatic colors, such as black, gray and brown, covering the canvas surface, he seemed to denounce the extreme cruelty of war. With his abstract expression of real life, he struck a resonant chord in viewers.

Park's "Protoplasm" series underwent a noticeable change in the 1970s. At that time, he was a professor at a college of fine arts with great influence on young artists as an avid proponent of the modern art movement. He supported up-and-coming artists and organized the Ecole de Seoul exhibition, while exhibiting unique abstract paintings based on innovative experimentation that differed from past works.

Park also freed himself from Western influences, blazing a new trail with his monochromatic abstract painting. This evolution was manifested in his "Ecriture" series, unveiled in the mid-1970s. This series, which he continues to explore today, was the start of monochrome abstract painting in Korea and an epoch-making effort to validate the identity of Korean modern art. "Ecriture" raises issues of the spiritual essence, not just matters of style or appearance. That is, it is an abstract expression that seeks to incorporate the artist's inner self into his painting techniques.

Park says that he "set out to have 'Ecriture' symbolize a monk meditating in a Seon (Zen) garden." Ultimately, his "Ecriture" is not a series of paintings on a one-dimensional surface, but conceptual art that "invites viewers into a place of meditation." In fact, these works have carved out a new niche in Korean modern art and enhanced its identity. In his early "Ecriture" works, Park covered the canvas in white and then applied an endless accumulation of lines, which created sculptural effects on the canvas, with the flat surface being transformed into a three- or four-dimensional spiritual space, or "a realm of meditation."

Park explained: "I wanted to emphasize emptiness more than fullness through the line drawings that fill the canvas. Art is no longer a task of filling something but a task of emptying something, and thus must involve throwing yourself away. Art must no longer reign over people, it must comfort people. Art that is filled by emptying yourself is the healing art that I seek."

Monochromatic tones, such as white, gray and pale yellow, form a space that can be filled because of its emptiness. If Western monochrome abstract painting deals with the characteristics of things and an expansion of space, then Park's "Ecriture" utilizes white space, which signifies an emptiness of the material with a spiritual space and autonomous "meditation realm." In Park's monochromatic painting viewers can discern a modern artistic identity that can be differentiated from that of the West.

"Ecriture" has undergone various stylistic changes during its 30-year existence that remains ongoing today. The early works, which were drawn in pencil on a white background, have long been superseded by a spiritual expression of matter that introduced the unique matière effects of traditional Korean paper. Spiritual expressions of the temporal and material are emphasized over movement. Above all, the matière of Korean paper and changes in colors lead viewers into a new realm of meditation. The non-finality of action, along with variances in surface texture and color, bring to mind the immateriality of accumulated materials. The density of space intensifies as materiality and the self come into harmony.

Park has sought of late to focus his attention on the issue of "healing art." He says: "Art must no longer burden the viewer. In the information age, the digital age of the 21st century, art must not dictate but instead soothe the viewer. My work method for this is to naturally achieve harmony between material and immaterial, like pouring ink onto the drawing paper."

1 "Ecriture No. 42-78-79-82" (1982)
Pencil and oil on hemp cloth, 194 x 259 cm
2 "Ecriture No. 37-75-76" (1976)
Pencil and oil on canvas, 194.5 x 300 cm

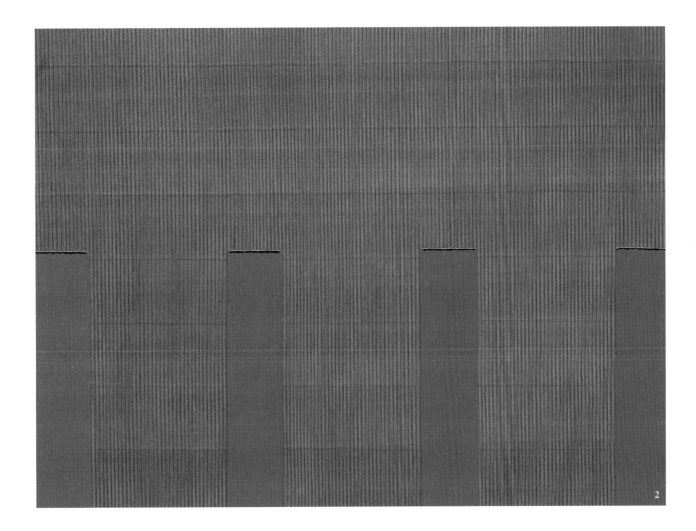

2

Recently, his works have been characterized by a move away from achromatic colors in favor of neutral colors, such as pale pink, faint blue, and gray. He calls these the "delicate neutral colors that are discovered in a life at the bottom." Muted monochromatic colors, without brilliance or intensity, are used to facilitate healing in modern life. His latest creations, which feature the concepts of emptiness and healing, include sculptural elements like a relief work. This demands participation of the viewer, who needs to view his works, not only from the front but also from the side to realize a formative change. While maintaining the basic requisites of painting, Park tries to stimulate the viewer's tactile experience with a variety of colors and forms, which are applied to create sculptural effects on the flat canvas surface. The stimulus to sight and touch contributes to a sense of comfort and familiarity. In this way, the viewer fills the emptiness and enters a realm of meditation that can heal a wounded heart.

Interestingly, Park admits: "In the past, my hands were nothing but tools used to achieve an end. And those works that relied on these hands as tools were sometimes distorted into handicraft or decorative works. Now I want to bring to life the touch of my hands." Park Seo-bo, a pioneer of Korean modern art, is thus endeavoring to create works that reflect his artistic essence and can manifest a "healing art" in keeping with the demands of the 21st century.

Yoo Jae-kil Art Critic / Professor of Art Studies, Hongik University

Lee Jong-sang
An Endless Quest for Origins of Form

1 "Protocontinent" (1970)
  Contemporary mural, 87 x 87 cm
2 "Dokdo – Energy II" (1982)
  Ink on Korean mulberry paper, 89 x 89 cm

L ee Jong-sang, born in 1938 in Yesan, Chung-cheongnam-do Province, majored in Oriental painting at the College of Fine Arts of Seoul National University. Lee made a sensational debut in 1962 when he became the youngest-ever artist recommended to participate in the Grand Art Exhibition of Korea, an annual competition organized by the Korean Fine Arts Association to discover new talent. In the 1970s and 1980s he studied comparative aesthetics and Eastern philosophy and received his Ph.D. from Dongguk University, the first such academic distinction earned by a painter in Korea. Thereafter, Lee has devoted his efforts to an exploration of modern expression based on traditional Korean ink painting.

As an artist, Lee is a rarity for his technical skills and theoretical concepts. His contributions to Korea's contemporary art over the past 50 years have been so immense that proper appreciation of his work is essential for understanding the trials and tribulations that modern Korean painting has experienced. From early on, Lee honed his skills in the manner of a soul-searching ascetic, while through his art he has constantly questioned his raison d'être as a Korean.

"Origins of Form 90073 – Longing for Reunification" (1990)
Ink and natural dyes on mulberry paper, 117 x 70 cm

Lee said: "I hoped to resolve at least two issues related to Korean contemporary painting. First, I wanted to find a new source of energy that transcends the tradition-bound limitations of Korean painting; and second, in response to the contemporary art trends that blindly followed Western modernism, I tried to develop a new concept of autogenesis as an alternative to heterogenesis."

In this case, autogenesis refers to a sense of identity based on the fundamental traditions of Korean art. According to Lee, art is intended for a self-development process, which should not be shaped by external factors or imitation. Along with advocating that an autonomous and independent school of Korean art needs to be established, he claims that the dominant traditions of past eras have influenced Korean painting of today, and will continue to do so in the future.

Lee's passion and philosophical outlook have compelled him to delve into the problems of contemporary Korean art, even as he worked on the creation of his own artistic world. His noteworthy accomplishments are the fruit of such lifelong endeavors.

Lee's art, spanning over a 50-year period, is centered around three styles: the *jingyeong* (true view landscape) style of realism, "new murals," and works that focus on the origins of form.

From the late Joseon Dynasty (1392–1910) through today, Korean landscape paintings have highlighted "true view," with a focus on realism. From the time when Lee first encountered this genre, he sought to understand the inherent characteristics of Korean landscape paint-

ing, which led to his immersion in the study of realism for more than two decades from 1959. While ignoring abstract notions, he rendered his observations of scenes of mountains, rocky cliffs, the sea and construction sites, in realistic detail, in ink and color on rice paper.

Lee's goal was to follow in the footsteps of Jeong Seon (1676–1759), the foremost master of true view landscape painting of the late Joseon period, to see for himself the mountains and waters of Korea, in an effort to interpret "true view landscape" from a contemporary Korean perspective. In particular, he sought to express the geomantic energy and earthly spirit of the Korean peninsula through his paintings of Dokdo.

"Of all my true-view style landscapes, I am especially fond of my paintings of Dokdo, the island in the East Sea," Lee said. "I have painted many interesting places around Korea, but Dokdo is the one place that has appealed to me most since the 1970s as the subject of my

art. Better than any other place, Dokdo reveals the dual forces of the spirit of the Earth, which is at the very heart of Korean-style landscape painting."

Lee's paintings of the "new mural" type can be grouped into three phases. The first phase is represented by such works as "Ancient Times" (1968–69), "Neungyeon" (1968), "Protocontinent" (1970) and "Twelve Symbols of Longevity and Blue Dragon" (1973); the second phase by "Origins of Form – From the Earth" (1989) and "Origins of Form – Longing for Reunification" (1990); and the third phase by the mural "Origins of a Form – Longing for Reunification" (1994). In particular, he sought to recreate, in a modern style, the archetypes associated with the collective symbols featured in the ancient tomb murals of the Goguryeo Kingdom (37 B.C.–A.D. 668). These works are characterized by his experimentation with various techniques, from ink and color painting to fresco, natural pigments, and oil painting on copper plate.

In 1988, Lee shifted his focus to an exploration of the origins of form, in both his landscapes and murals, which served to reinforce his artistic philosophy. Until 1995, his endeavors were mostly of a distinctive style that combined the light touches of ink painting with the relatively heavier tones of color painting, using ink and light color and natural pigments on traditional Korean materials, such as *jangji*, a thick, durable paper. As for his subject matter, he often depicted the images of a divisive society. After 1995, he studied the origins of form, producing works along the lines of Korean archaism, employing the Earth as the quintessential form.

After inventing his own style of oil painting, in which ink and natural pigments are spontaneously applied to mulberry paper, Lee reached the zenith of his artistic career. Through his paintings, he sought to criticize the absurdities of the times, while expressing his desire to piece together the emotional and existential fragments resulting from the absurd situation surrounding the divided Korean peninsula. In stark contrast to his earlier works, these paintings seemed to reflect an attempt to bring symbolic redemption to reality by imbuing his works with a Catholic spirit.

An overarching concept of Lee's works can be defined by the German term *urform*, prototype or "original form." This concept embodies and speaks for his entire oeuvre, while the art of his lifetime could be summarized in such simple words as "autogenesis" and "pre-figures."

Lee explains: "With the concept of autogenesis, I wanted to criticize heterogenesis. Traditional Korean painting is a typical example of heterogeneous art that was born out of cross-breeding with Chinese painting. It represented a style of painting that was created by blindly accepting the views of nature and conservative styles based on the Confucio-Mencian mindset and the doctrines of Zhu Xi, which were applied to the landscape

"I hoped to resolve at least two issues related to Korean contemporary painting. First, I wanted to find a new source of energy that transcends the tradition-bound limitations of Korean painting; and second, in response to the contemporary art trends that blindly followed Western modernism, I tried to develop a new concept of autogenesis as an alternative to heterogenesis."

1 "Twelve Symbols of Longevity and Blue Dragon" (1973)
   Canvas mural, 287 x 405 cm
2 "Origins of Form 89117 – From the Earth" (1989)
   Copper glaze mural, 400 x 1,300 cm

painting of Korea."

Along with making known his critical views, Lee also sought to secure a theoretical foundation to differentiate his art from Chinese painting through autogenesis. His views were not about an ideology of nationalism. Rather, he wanted to emphasize the necessity of establishing an identity that Korean contemporary painting could pursue in the face of today's regionalization. By propounding "autogenesis," he wanted to warn that Korean art should not stray from the characteristic form and quality of Korean culture.

"Pre-figures" make up another element of Lee's art, which suggest that, as long as a painting remains what it is, it must embody historical "fore-context." No matter how boundless freedom artists can enjoy, they cannot ignore their historical and social roots; therefore, Lee contends, a painting without a fore-context will not only lose its identity but its nationality as well.

"True art cannot come out of either arbitrariness or nothingness. This is why I seek to reveal historical reality in my works. I try to derive this spirit from Dokdo and the Goguryeo murals, and have devoted my life to portraying it in my work. All my true-view depictions of Dokdo, which are based on the geomantic principles, and my wall paintings, all inspired by the Goguryeo tomb murals, are the result of my attempt to embody this reality," Lee said.

Lee's art is a manifestation of his exploration of the origins of the Korean form. His art can be likened to a discovery of sunken treasure after a lengthy search of the vast sea of Korea's geography and history. As such, his paintings not only preserve the bold, simple and subtle beauty of Korean art, but also serve to reinterpret with a modern sensibility the unique Korean aesthetics of incompletion and margin, and the concepts of artlessness and unconventionality.

Kim Bok-yeong Art Critic / Professor, Hongik University

Lim Ok-sang

Between the Everyday and the Monumental

1 "Dream of Steel I" (2001)
Scrap steel, spoons and knives; 130 x 230 cm
2 "Mother Earth" (1993)
Iron, 335 x 210 cm

Lim Ok-sang is known as an artist deeply involved in pro-democracy struggle. After completing his undergraduate and graduate art degrees in Seoul, Lim attended the Fine Arts School of Angouleme from 1984 to 1986, the first Korean to study at the internationally recognized art school in southwestern France.

Lim recalls, "While I was away in France, the waves of democratization were beginning to sweep over Korea, leading toward far-reaching changes though under harsh pressure by President Chun Doo-hwan's military regime. I felt sad and frustrated to be absent at such a critical time. I thought that if I could only return to take part in those events, I would gladly give up my art…"

Strong words — but he was at heart an artist. His artistic spirit, something close to an instinct lodged deep within his body, could not be denied.

The artist goes on, "There is a beautiful little chateau on a hill, and below it stretch broad plains with a river running through them. What had been a cigarette factory was remodeled into an art school, and that is where I painted 'A Modern History of Africa.'

"The French tradition in art is of course superb, but having come from Korea, I felt I had to show them some-

1

2

thing different. The other students thought I was strange at first, but they gradually started to nod their heads and seemed to feel a powerful attraction. Perhaps it was that after searching for a new direction in contemporary art through problems of form and technique, they were overwhelmed by this Third World content and the strength of form that it produced."

"A Modern History of Africa" was approved by the Académie Française and subsequently exhibited in the United States. Lim recalls that a curator or a critic involved in organizing the exhibition wrote more or less as follows: "Many Third World artists try to gain exposure in the West by choosing subjects of 'social activism,' but Lim Ok-sang's 'A Modern History of Africa' does something different. Although this work does indeed depict the modern history of Africa, it achieves a beauty of form that transcends its subject."

It is my belief that every great artist retains in his memory a scene from the time he first viewed the world in artistic terms. A scene that the artist saw is condensed in a process of "scene = story," and whenever the artist recalls it, the original pleasure will return.

"I have memories about the Korean War and my family. When I heard that someone had given birth to a stillborn child, I fell under the illusion that I was ill. And I thought that being ill was really beautiful. I was a timid and well-behaved child. When faced with the dark or the unknown, I must have felt torn between curiosity and fear, or even terror."

Let's stop the story here for now, because I am more interested in the "scene = story" equation than in the story itself. It is through this equation that the scene or the scenification of war and family and the stillborn child became the motifs of Lim's barley field painting series (pitting nature against civilization, hometown against memories of war, insecurity against impulse, realism against modernism, desire against repulsion, and the shapes of primary colors against the primary colors of shapes), or his family series in paper relief (whereby the depth of time is deftly though paradoxically expressed by the thinness of paper, the eternity beyond the tragedy of history by a deathlike dilution of life), or his Maehyang-ri series (whose human forms, assembled from the scrap iron of spent bomb shells gathered from the U.S. Air Force firing range at Maehyang-ri, transcend their "Anti-American" theme through an opera buffa aesthetic of death-cum-laughter). And the "scene = story" is all the more interesting for being more artistic than narrative.

When it comes to the mixture of curiosity and fear, or even terror, toward the unknown, the "scene = story = aesthetic" that these triple series embrace, though historical, mobilizes a deepening and enlivening of history to attain the universality of "art = being." It is at this point in art that the everyday and the monumental come to coexist, become interdependent, and heighten each other, ultimately emerging as two sides of the same coin.

Now, let's listen to the rest of the story. How does a scene get scenified?

"My elementary school was on a hill in the upper reaches of the Baengma River, and below the hill the river flowed. I had to walk 3 kilometers to school along mountain paths, and the river and the hills changed strikingly with the seasons. I have a vivid memory of going on a picnic when I was in first grade. It was April, and a haze hovered over the ploughed fields, and although the trees had been cut short by bombing, they were starting to put out new green shoots."

This scene of nature's regeneration overcoming the wounds of war, of the moist earth becoming one with life, leads us to a dramatic speech that despairs, to the contrary, of the death latent within this burgeoning of life:

"The hills in May are as healthy as a great herd of galloping deer…the corpses in the Elbe River…"

These lines from Wolfgang Borchert's "*Draußen vor der Tür*" (The Man Outside), a play that starkly portrays the despair and alienation of the defeated soldiers returning to Germany at the end of World War II, culminate in the following *cri de coeur* by the hero Beckmann:

You who affirm, where are you now? Answer me! I need you, you who answer! Where can you be? You've disappeared all of a sudden! Where are you, you who forbid me to die, where are you? Where is that old man who called himself God? Why doesn't he answer? But the answer! Why are they silent? Why? Then, is there no answer? No answer at all? Then is there no answer, none at all…

In his college days, Lim was heavily involved in theater. He was a good actor, too. During the dark years of President Park Chung-hee's "Yusin" dictatorship, he avoided surrendering to pessimism by doing just what he was to do in his later life in whatever field he turned his hand to: he did not so much make art out of dramatic subjects as he made the dramatic aesthetic the very life and blood of his art. For the dramatic aesthetic is the most constructive, corporeal, and optimistic. To this day, in Lim's art, even the smallest and most static element is at the same time dynamic, and this dynamism is the very core of traditional drama. It was probably because of this quality that Lim,

"A Modern History of Africa – Part I: The African Continent" (1984), 5,000 x 150 cm

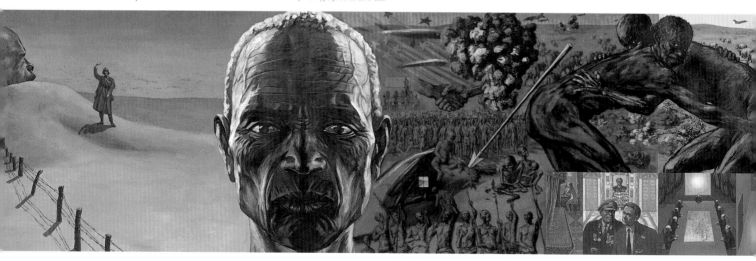

even while moving from his beginnings as a painter in Korea of the 1970s to an increasingly activist stance, was able to avoid the dogma of "*minjung* (the people) = subject" and create a form appropriate to "*minjung* = contents."

"Before I read all those books in preparation for writing my graduate thesis, I had been suffering from the modern disease. I was constantly experimenting with new forms. But ultimately, these new forms were not mine: they had neither nationality nor individuality. And so I decided I must start again from scratch. I would not produce abstract paintings. I felt I must portray Korea's past and present, and not lose touch with our tradition."

What he created as a means of sharing these thoughts and putting them into practice was "Twelve Months Ago." Around this time the first politically critical artistic movement since the Korean War of the 1950s, Facts and Words, was founded in October 1979, shortly before the assassination of Park Chung-hee, when his dictatorial regime was reaching its peak. Lim played a leading role in establishing the group.

"Before Facts and Words, any social criticism was expressed in symbolic terms, but it became more direct. I believed that communication with society was the most important function of art, and I became more involved in activities outside of art. Or, to be more accurate, I was excited to be working together with other people and other artists. Meeting, organization — I liked these words. I had a great time getting together with Kim Yong-tae, Ju Jae-hwan, Min Joung-ki and Kang Yo-bae, to give rein to our 'hamming vein.'"

This "hamming vein" (*ttanttara gijil* — is this not a pure Korean equivalent of the Sino-Korean *yeongeuk mihak* or "dramatic aesthetic?") continued over the next 20 years through all of Lim's activities (including his participation in the environmental movement, the Korean unification movement, and a broader movement for world peace) as well as his works, deepening the dialectic between the two. And under the new presidency of Roh Moo-hyun, it is likely to be enlisted in a large-scale public art project.

Indeed, Lim's attachment to public art is something very special. It has produced diverse fruits stretching way back in his career. He has installed public art works in such locations as Gwanghwamun Station on Seoul's subway line No. 5; Gurim Village in Yeongam, Jeollanam-do Province; Maehyang-ri in Hwaseong County, Gyeonggi-do Province; and the Suwon World Cup Stadium. Since 1999 he has conducted a weekly popular art program, "You're an Artist Too," in Insa-dong and Yeouido Park.

"In the hands of the artist, the heavy metal body of an air-to-surface missile warhead, split in half lengthways, becomes the case of a sexy black hi-fi system with the sophisticated beauty and old-fashioned elegance of traditional wooden furniture (the conference table); or four shards of splintered bomb casings show their unaltered yet perfectly balanced contours beneath a glass top, as graceful as slender feminine limbs (the tea table)."

1 "Conference Table" (2002)
Shell casings from Maehyang-ri, aluminum, steel and glass; 70 x 90 x 210 cm
2 "Dream of Steel II" (2001)
Scrap steel, spoons and knives; 170 x 220 cm

Lim has so far worked mainly in the media of clay, paper and iron. What is his artistic perspective on these materials?

"Clay is soft, with a caressing quality. It feels comfortable, offering the widest surface area for us to touch… It has the admirable property of absorbing everything. Paper is organically related to clay. It might even be called a sort of purified clay. It's also related to the colors white and ivory, and although its possibilities are limited, that is part of its charm. I probably wouldn't have adopted iron had it not been for Maehyang-ri. At college, when I saw the sculpture students using oxyacetylene torches, I thought it was scary… But after all, I think it was my inevitable destiny to work with iron, although I'm now trying to come up with a strategy for the post-Iron Age…"

Doesn't his use of iron signify a pursuit of modernism, a modernism that includes the realism, not of the past, but of the future?

"Perhaps. But there is no need to label it as modernism. Sometimes I think it must be my temperament and my destiny to be always seeking out something new: a temperament and a destiny that is always despairing, yet always seeking."

When set against his artistic feeling for clay, paper and iron, how fascinating the artistic "scenification = story" of Lim's life becomes! But what about the terror of the unknown? At the end of a piece called "Chamber Music of Shattered Bombshells," which I wrote for Lim's recent exhibition, "Thinking after the Iron Age," I put it like this:

"But the highlight of this exhibition must surely be the "ultra-modern" furniture: tables, chairs, tea tables and conference tables made chiefly from the outer cases of bombshells. In the hands of the artist, the heavy metal body of an air-to-surface missile warhead, split in half lengthways, becomes the case of a sexy black hi-fi system with the sophisticated beauty and old-fashioned elegance of traditional wooden furniture (the conference table); or four shards of splintered bomb casings show their unaltered yet perfectly balanced contours beneath a glass top, as graceful as slender feminine limbs (the tea table).

That's it. It's the moment when the art of spatial compression, through the unexpected mediation of these bomb casings, becomes a chamber music of temporal compression. It's the scene that transforms the capitalism of the bomb, again through the unexpected mediation of the bomb's shell, into the socialism of art. Thanks to these works, the product of a qualitative fulfillment of the above processes, we can find something more than a slogan in the socialist motto, 'Let us melt down our swords to make ploughshares.'"

What is this if not an equation between the everyday and the monumental?

Kim Jeong-hwan Poet / Art Critic   **Lim Ok-sang Art Institute** Photographs

Paik Nam-june (Nam June Paik)
Progenitor of Multimedia Art

1

1 "The Tiger Lives" (2000)
A video art work featuring a cello and a traditional Korean string instrument called *wolgeum* (moon lute) by Paik Nam-june, installed in the lobby of the Seoul Art Gallery.
2 "East Gate" (1992)
Paik's video works create highly innovative artistic forms and content.

Paik Nam-june's attraction to video art is rooted in the versatility of electronic media, which was developed to efficiently disseminate information and be used by the general public. For this reason, Paik is far more closely connected with the masses than other artists who deal with traditional media such as painting and sculpture. He has created the globalized new art form of multimedia art. He utilizes commercial media technology as a tool to create his works, but he applies electronic media technology as a means to create a new artistic realm. Therefore, his artistic creations are intimately related to the human condition.

Paik Nam-june (Nam June Paik) endows electronic media with humane characteristics. Thus, through the structural meaning inherent in his works he has broadened the horizon of contemporary artistic expression and also expanded the scope of his own artistic expression. Paik's works constantly cause viewers to reflect upon the spiritual state of humanity and the nature of art.

Paik has endeavored to convey an understanding of electronic media through a human-centered worldview by highlighting various universal themes, such as religion and humanity, as major influences that shape the structural

2

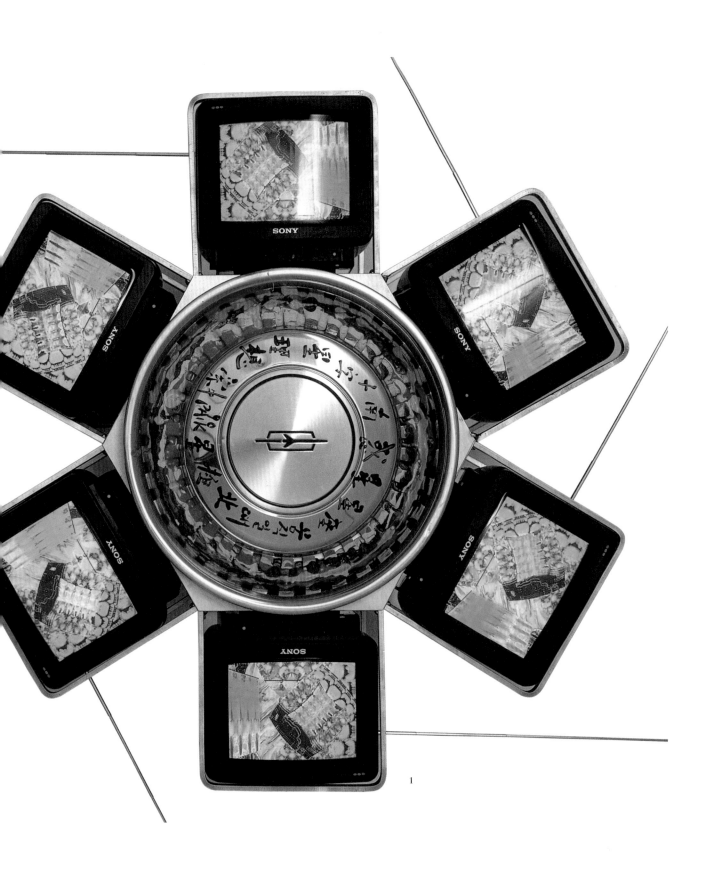

1

context of his works. He also incorporates the potential power of such fundamental elements as love, death and nature as structural modes in his work. However, Paik does not seek to dwell on causal relationships. By putting into practice his aesthetic response to technological media as a means of structure development, he maintains his distance from blind passion, including an unconditional devotion to artistic pursuit commonly seen in "art for art's sake." This is because the aesthetic concepts often seen in his diverse works can be understood as a search for identity related to his own origins and experiences. It is upon this foundation that the intertwining of time and space, and the blending of past (Korea) and present (the world) experiences, which can be easily found in his works, are symbolically reflected.

The flowing frames of the individual images in his video works play a role like that of the notes of a musical piece played by a musician. His visual music is metaphorically expressed through a dual structure of the simultaneous flow of time and the display of images. Therefore, if you were to listen to modern atonal music or 12-tone music while viewing the video images of his works, it would not be too difficult to grasp the similarities between his video works and modern Western music.

As a first-generation artist to use electronic media as a means of artistic expression, Paik cannot escape from being responsible for creating a link between the art of traditional media and this new art form. Paik draws on Buddha, Korean shamans, and related religious icons for his works and performances, thereby connecting tradition

with modern technology. He continuously varies his artistic icons and adapts them to new environments through his works. This metaphysical approach to art seems to be a natural outcome based on his choice of television and video media. The virtual realm that Paik created through his video art heralded the birth of contemporary multimedia art. He merged imagery created through electronic signals with pure art tradition. In the context of art history, he discovered and expanded the aesthetic potential of multimedia art. In particular, this can be more readily seen when viewed from a context of his works — sculptural form — that is, "video sculpture." Through his video works, Paik presented a new art form and content, while prominently distinguishing his works as among the most revolutionary forms in the history of art.

For example, as a representative work that fundamentally changed art and human perception, Paik's "TV Buddha" (1974) foretold the emergence of modern two-way communication. In this work, the Buddha meditates on his own image, reproduced electronically on a monitor. Among the teachings of the Buddha is this insightful passage: "All things in this world are forms without substance, but each of those forms make up the substance of this world; forms exist only temporarily, and there is no substance." Accordingly, the Buddha does not make a distinction between existence and non-existence, and therefore he would not say that the image appearing on the TV screen is not his actual self. This sort of equal relationship between the image of existence and the existence itself implies that there is no difference between image and reality, such that the barrier between art and non-art is transcended, while spatially invigorating the area around the work.

The space between the Buddha and the monitor is transformed into a sphere of dynamic energy, which can be seen as a metaphor for an evolution of modern art whereby non-artistic elements are now critical aspects that form the foundation of art. The concept of "introducing commonality into works of art," which became an important topic of discussion during the time of Marcel Duchamp in the early 20th century, can be interpreted as a more positive notion of "bringing art to the level of everyday living." However, a more significant point is that through "TV Buddha" Paik was able to expand the scope of his aesthetic form. He also advanced the possibility of mutual exchange between the spirit and the material, and

Because Paik deals with electronic media within the artistic tradition, the paradoxical modes which arise — that is, the new art form of video art that becomes possible through the merger of technology and human modes such as love or religion — have become a prototype for 20th century art works that present a new direction for contemporary art.

notably extended the epistemological horizon of his artistic expression. The virtual realm created by Paik through electronic media technology and its applications led to the advent of modern multimedia art. He fused the imagery he created through electronic signals not with pure art itself, but with its traditional languages and artistic concepts. By integrating traditional art forms and the new video media in his video sculptures, Paik brought together existence (sculpture) and non-existence (video imagery).

Because Paik deals with electronic media within the artistic tradition, the paradoxical modes which arise — that is, the new art form of video art that becomes possible through the merger of technology and human modes such as love or religion — have become a prototype for 20th century art works that present a new direction for contemporary art.

As he boldly omits narrative modes from his video works and expresses incidental moments, Paik creates noteworthy contemporary and avant-garde artistic modes that dramatize the artistic situation itself. Along with this point of view, he creates the common sense current in late capitalistic society, which emphasizes self-identity or the importance of non-existence through the media and themes of his works. In that he envisions such a new hope for the future, we may expect him to assume a leadership role among artists.

Paik also demonstrates, through the artistic expressions which begin with his insight to integrate humanity with the new nature of technology, that his synthesis of technology and humanity form a new perspective. Also, his development of a harmonious relationship between the human spirit and the reality of life disrupted by a highly individualized culture has been possible because of the artist.

The complementarity of existence and non-existence in Paik's works is the first step toward a virtual reality that facilitates the fundamental principle of interactivity in multimedia art. That is, the epistemological equivalence of image and reality creates works of art not based on the material, but rather the immaterial aspects based on images. Therefore, viewers are not just passively observing that which is being presented; they participate in the completion of the existence of a work that represents an environment. And so the viewer becomes a part of the work, and can also control it. While objectifying the work, viewers may also be able to develop a relationship between life and art in ways different from that of traditional works of art.

Jeong Yong-do Art Critic **Kim Kwang-su** Photographer

Choi Man-lin

Simple Forms Express Universal Sentiments

"O" [07-3-01] (2007)
Bronze, 83 x 65 x 165 cm

Sculptor Choi Man-lin's childhood may be described as a time of extreme pain and suffering. Born in 1935, during the period of Japanese colonial rule, he experienced the social upheaval of tumultuous times in the country's modern history: Japanese oppression, national liberation, the division of the Korean peninsula, despotism, and the Korean War. Naturally, all this while, his foremost concern was survival. Nevertheless, he was relatively more fortunate than his parents, who spent the better years of their lives under colonial rule, without even the freedom to speak their mother tongue. After the nation regained independence, Choi enrolled at Kyunggi Middle School, one of the country's most prestigious schools. Graduates of Kyunggi Middle and High School included a number of renowned artists, such as the video artist Paik Nam-june (Nam June Paik) and *gayageum* (12-string zither) player Hwang Byung-ki.

Choi was inspired to pursue a career in art by his teacher Park Seung-gu, who had been mentored by Kim Bok-jin, a pioneer of Korean modern sculpture and a graduate of the Tokyo Academy of Fine Arts. Sensing the artistic talent of his student, Park sought to nurture Choi into a sculptor. Choi remembers his teacher as being thoughtful and attentive. He recalled, "During a modeling lesson, I was careless and a clump of clay fell onto the floor. He came to me quietly and picked it up. Then he told me, 'Think of clay as your own flesh and handle it with care.' Under my teacher's guidance, I could dream of becoming a sculptor."

In 1949, when he was just 14 years old, Choi submitted a work to the first Korean National Fine Arts Exhibition. And when his sculpture, "Face," received an award, it attracted much public attention. His formal education as a sculptor began with his enrollment at Seoul National University in 1954. To comply with the wishes of his

1 "O" [04-5-01] (2004)
   Bronze, 33 x 30 x 27 cm
2 "O" [07-4-01] (2007)
   Bronze, 50 x 32 x 38 cm

parents, he first applied to the Department of Economics; however, he later changed his mind to follow his dream, and transferred to the College of Fine Arts. In 1958, he received a Bachelor of Fine Arts degree in sculpture. From 1956, while still a college student, Choi began exhibiting his sculptural works, such as "Autumn" and "Woman," at the Korean National Fine Arts Exhibition (1956), and "Mother and Son" at the same exhibition the following year. In particular, "Mother and Son" showed an emphasis on the linear form, rather than three-dimensional features, through a simplified representation of slender figures. The focus on emotional attachment, which is characteristic of Choi's works, is also evident in his "Eve" series created in 1958 and thereafter. With a kind of primitive nature, which combines delicacy with substance, each work in the series expresses the artist's appreciation of life as well as his bewilderment and anxiety about the times.

The "Eve" series was not inspired by Western contemporary sculpture; rather, it is rooted in primitive art forms. In the early days of his artistic career, Choi was influenced by the "Venus of Willendorf," a Paleolithic stone statuette discovered in 1909 at an archaeological site along the Danube River in Austria. The figurine is thought to have served as a symbol of abundance and fecundity. In stark contrast to the implications of its name, "Venus," the figure is far from beautiful from modern aesthetic standpoints. It has no facial features but only nominal arms and

no feet, while the body parts related to reproduction are exponentially exaggerated, suggesting its role related to fertility. Similarly, Choi's "Eve" series highlights the basic essence of human life.

The works in the series are characterized by textures that optimize the properties of clay. Though each work ignores the mainstream concepts of Western-style classical sculpture, such as harmony, symmetry and proportion, they project powerful life energy by revealing the primordial nature of clay. The rugged surfaces and distorted forms, with parts randomly lopped off, seem to represent the fundamental human existence devoid of redundancy. They exude a great sense of relief, as if freed from a state of extreme anxiety or tension. This might be Choi's way of expressing the state of human existence.

However, Choi is hesitant to acknowledge any such abstruse interpretation. He notes: "It is an emotional extravagance to describe these works, created out of the desperate need to survive through the difficult times I had to endure, with highly abstract concepts like existentialism or ontology. Nevertheless, these works are meaningful for their existence alone and the potential to bring about change in our notion of beauty."

His choice of the title "Eve" has little to do with religion. He thinks of Eve not as the mother of humankind, as depicted in the Bible, but rather as a universal human who is destined to suffer from the original sin of a worldly existence. In this sense, Eve is also a manifestation of Choi's personal struggles during a dark period of Korea's modern history. Likewise, his works show that he is less interested in aesthetic expression of the human body than in an exploration of the essence of the human condition.

About the time when Choi embarked on his artistic career, Korea was only beginning to recover from the utter devastation of the Korean War. People had to wage a hellish struggle for mere survival in the harsh reality. In his "Eve" series, however, Choi sought to convey his refusal to give up hope, despite such dire circumstances, as well as his optimism for recovery. In this way, the series represents a reconstructive, rather than deconstructive, process of human endurance, reflecting his artistic sensibilities.

Influences of the nation's traditional culture are also obvious in Choi's works. This includes his efforts to appreciate the identity of Korean art, as reflected in his master's thesis on Korean traditional masks, and the ways in which his subsequent works, after the "Eve" series, incorporated principles of Eastern thought regarding humankind and the universe.

Although the title of a work does not necessarily define its meaning, Choi's works from this period — "Heaven" (1965), "Earth" (1965), "Darkness" (1966), "Yellow" (1967), "Yin" (1969) and "Yang" (1969), and the series "Sun and Moon" and "Placenta" — all represent his attempts to return to Korea's cultural roots and shift his emphasis from antagonism to reconciliation. In a transition to abstract sculpture, his works began to feature more fundamental and philosophical themes. For

2

He has sought to explore the subtle elegance of Korean folk art, the essence of calligraphic forms, and the forms that can express universal sentiments on the basis of Eastern principles. This approach is the result of his refusal to indulge in fleeting trends, while striving to infuse his aesthetic language with Korean culture.

example, he sought to express the restrained but potent vibrancy of Oriental calligraphy. In the "Sun and Moon" series, which portrays abstract images of Korean totem poles, Choi approached abstract art from a point of view that deviated from influences of the West.

In particular, his efforts were concentrated on three-dimensional renderings of the brush strokes of calligraphic characters. Choi explained: "While feeling uncertain about the direction of my work, I visited a calligraphy exhibition and discovered the unique beauty of the ancient script. All of a sudden, I decided to create the strokes in three-dimensional forms, which resulted in this series."

While being inspired by one of the most ancient forms of Korean art, he adopted original applications to his sculptural works. But he was not indifferent to the trends of contemporary art nor did he reject them outright. Rather, he sought to create an artistic language of his own. Thereafter, he created the "Placenta" series, featuring forms that resembled human organs. The forms, however, are not simply replications of body parts; they represent the human body as a microcosm of the universe and the cycle of life.

With a deepened respect for the dignity of human life, he realized that life is much more than physical existence but involves a more fundamental and transcendental realm. This realization led him to further simplify his forms, as represented by his "O" series, with a hollowed out interior within a well-defined outline. His recent works, which are all titled "O," typically take the shape of a globular form. The ambiguity of the title "O" can refer to beginning or end, absence or presence, the finite or the infinite.

As Choi explained, the title "could be interpreted as the number zero, the 'non-existence' in Taoism, or the 'emptiness' (*sunyata*) of Buddhism. 'O' can even mean the

Pythagorean Monad, the symbol that Greek philosophers used to refer to the true nature of things."

Being simple yet distinctively defined, his globular forms symbolize a source of existence, something vast enough to embrace the universe. Moreover, these works are notably inclusive in that they are open to various interpretations, though Choi himself resists any kind of conceptualization. Like untitled pieces of music, each work of the "O" series does not have a title so as to not restrict its intrinsic character.

Choi seems to adopt a new theme roughly every decade. However, this does not mean that he merely exploits a single basic pattern throughout a 10-year period. He has rejected any form of categorization, along with preferring to work alone. Every 10 years or so, he has established a structural framework and then later demolished it with a thorough, if not painful, process of self-transformation.

He has sought to explore the subtle elegance of Korean folk art, the essence of calligraphic forms, and the forms that can express universal sentiments on the basis of Eastern principles. This approach is the result of his refusal to indulge in fleeting trends, while striving to infuse his aesthetic language with Korean culture.

Choi's love for the nation's indigenous art motivated him to organize a series of exhibitions of early modern Korean art while he was serving as director of the National Museum of Contemporary Art. He does not present a grand vision about the future direction of Korean art. Rather, he continues to listen to his inner voice and to contemplate the world around him. His recent works express an "aesthetic of emptiness," which embraces the universe with the simplest forms possible.

Choi Tae-man Art Critic **Ahn Hong-beom** Photographer

"Eve" (1965)
Gypsum, 35 x 35 x 80 cm
© Leeum, Samsung Museum of Art

Ahn Kyu-chul

Conceptual Mediator of Objects and Language

Ahn Kyu-chul has led Korea's conceptual art scene since the 1980s with works that combine photography, drawing and writing. He has thus built up a unique body of work that manages to fuse a critical view of reality and the conceptuality of language, two elements that do not seem to readily complement each other. With visual restraint, Ahn's works stimulate an intellectual association of ideas, which uncovers the contradictions of today's society with a fusion of objects with minimal illusion and a delicate language.

"I have this habit of constantly doubting art even as I create it. As the producer of handcrafted images, I feel a sense of helplessness in the face of the vast power of a flood of images, and I am skeptical about the role of art in the real world that is ruled by money and economics. As I work with images, I presage their suspicious nature that hides and distorts reality," says Ahn.

For Ahn, this means taking art beyond sensibility and making it a clear expression of intellect. In other words, art is not sensed through sight and touch, but instead is an object and a language that can be understood through intelligent thought. In a sense, this has become the mainstream direction of contemporary art and its way out. The platonic love for immaterialism offered by conceptual art transforms a work of art so that it is not simply an artistic creation but also a medium and a language for communication. If a critical statement is added, art is no longer about the material but becomes a grammatical system that involves oral and written communication.

Sculpture can never be completely free from objects and language, since it is highly material and lyrical at the same time. If so, which Korean artist has transformed the prosaic language of objects in everyday life into a poetic spiritual language, and who has managed to go beyond abstraction that simply removes the physical shape to

"Hat" (1994)
380 x 1,200 cm
A portrayal of the cruelty of human relationships: only a hat remains of one individual who has been devoured by another according to the law of the jungle.

"People who make art have an obsession with hand labor. But the things that I make are not the doors or the pillars. I make empty space, the void. It disappears when the exhibition ends but it remains inside the minds of the viewers."

"Room with 112 Doors" (2003–2004)
760 x 760 x 230 cm
Doors that fail to function as barriers between the inside and the outside become a symbolic manifestation of insecurity: All kinds of potential threat can enter a room with too many doors.

achieve a truly conceptual language? I would say it is Ahn Kyu-chul, without hesitation.

Ahn, who is known as a "thinking sculptor" and "interpreter of objects," held a large-scale exhibition that ran for almost two months last year. A kind of mini-retrospective event, which was presented at the Rodin Gallery (March 5–April 25, 2004), it featured three old installations combining text and objets d'art — "The Man's Suitcase," "Hat" and "Man who Disappeared Into the Box" — alongside three new works: "Unshakable Room," "Bottomless Room" and "Room with 112 Doors."

Those who know about Ahn's debut and how he works might have wondered how the artist would deal with such an expansive and formal space as the Rodin Gallery. Ahn embarked on his artistic journey in a humble manner with papier-mâché, a light and cheap material that was said to be "of the people," mainly for housewives and children who visited cultural centers.

Ahn said: "I began in the 1980s with works that were called 'story sculptures' or 'landscape sculptures.' From 1983 to 1986 I made a series of works that featured finger-sized figures in miniature tableaus satirizing current events or political situations. I did this kind of work because I didn't like the way existing sculpture pursued perfection of handiwork while immersed in a discourse of pure art and shut off from the contradictions of the world outside. With my 'story sculptures,' made of papier-mâché and plaster, I tried to make 'light' sculpture that minimized the physical labor of the artist and the material substance of standard sculpture. At the time it fell in with the spirit of *minjung* art (people's art) in some ways, but I could not help distancing myself from the moral gravity that was prevalent in the minjung art movement and the artist-centered attitude."

Ahn's distancing himself from minjung art and the artist-centered attitude became more apparent in his 1992

solo exhibition, held after he returned home from studying in Germany. Members of the minjung art fraternity, Reality and Utterance, and other colleagues criticized his work as "philosophy of objects" and "German-style work," while to traditional sculptors his work was not "formative art but the play of conceptual ideas." However, it is worth nothing that he was lauded and embraced by the younger art critics. The exhibition created quite a stir, which served as a catalyst that accelerated Ahn's transformation.

"My work changed greatly while I was overseas (1987–1995)," Ahn said. "I was seriously worried that my work did not go much further than social cartoons in three-dimensional form. I felt I had reached the limit in terms of finding a framework for certain sculptural scenes, and how to depict things in descriptive ways. While contemplating materiality and three-dimensionality, the fundamental elements of sculpture, my interest moved from the social environment surrounding people to the objects made by people. A turning point in my work came when I began to focus on the fact that everyday objects reflect the thoughts and relations of people. My focus shifted from a macroscopic view of 'between people' to a microscopic view of 'between things,' and I began to look at implication and paradox rather than narrative description of a situation. The method of utterance in my works changed from a narrative of 'doing…' to a question of 'why do…'"

Ahn's work can be seen to have developed through four phases: narrative illustration-style sculpture; exploration of the relationship between speech and objects; stories that depict a fairy tale or cartoon-like imagination; and large-scale room and house series of works. A common thread seen in all his works is a characteristic that makes his works a kind of mise-en-scene, or "theater of sculpture" — a rejection of the spectacular element invariably found in today's sculpture and resulting super-realistic utterance of the imagination — with minimal elements.

"My objets d'art works of the early 1990s were the outcome of such changes. The typical motifs in my works were doors, jackets, shoes, glasses, hammers, tablecloths, blackboards and chairs. The hammer as a tool of destruction appears under the name of love, a shoe brush becomes a personified being with self-consciousness who repents 'sin,' and the blackboard acquires such a strong sense of self that it abandons its original function. In this process, letters are introduced as a part of the objets, and cartoon elements have been introduced in the works 'Hat' (1994) and 'The Man's Suitcase.'"

A noteworthy aspect of Ahn's work is the way he reverses the ready-made approach of French artist Marcel Duchamp. Whereas Duchamp presented ready-made articles that were made to appear like handcrafts, Ahn presents handcrafts that are like ready-made articles.

"People who make art have an obsession with hand labor. But the things that I make are not the doors or the

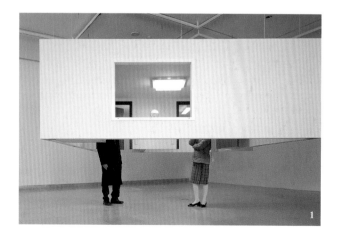

1 "Bottomless Room" (2004)
    540 x 360 x 122 cm
    A room with no floor represents the instability of the lives of people who seem to drift about aimlessly, never putting down roots.
2 "Unshakable Room" (2004)
    660 x 570 x 380 cm
    A paradoxical expression of how strenuously people try to hold onto things that are disappearing.

2

pillars. I make empty space, the void. It disappears when the exhibition ends but it remains inside the minds of the viewers. I sometimes borrow the form of ready-made objects but I have no interest in modifying them to turn them into precious art objects. By recreating these items as they are, I try to divest them of their aura. I don't want to create an aura, but rather, discard any aura. You could say I am aiming not for a simple arrangement of ready-made things but for nothingness."

Thus Ahn strives to dilute the flavoring of his formative language, or he seems intent to concentrate on cooking with the object itself being the main ingredient. He adapts a neutral style found in the "zero degree" writing advocated by Roland Barthes, or the nouveau Roman style of writing.

Every sculpture involves an object and a language. It has a physical form that cannot easily overcome its linguistic structure and context of communication. But the language is too often corrupted and overdone. In light of such circumstances, Ahn seeks to focus on: "How can the artist restore the pureness of the language?" He has finally come to realize that suppressing the most material element means sublimating the most spiritual essence. The sublimation of material art, to transform art into ideology and then transcend it, is at the core of conceptual art, and it is this vastness of conceptual art that provides the power and authority to thwart or satirize the absurdity of reality.

The seen and the known, heaviness and lightness, critical themes and surreal imagination, the native language of art and foreign languages — few artists endeavor to create a balance between all of these aspects as Ahn Kyu-chul does. As such, there should be no question about Ahn's standing as Korea's foremost conceptual artist.

Lee Ken-shu Senior Editor, Monthly Art (*Wolganmisool*)
Choi Hang-young, Rodin Gallery Photography

Lee Hyung-koo
A Post-Human Dr. Jekyll's Eerie Reality

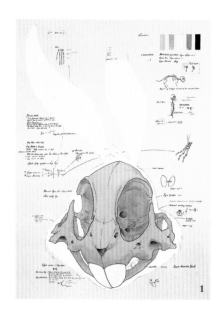

1 "A01" (2005)
   Pencil, ink, marker and acrylic on paper; 109 x 79 cm
2 "Anas Animatus D" (2006)
   Resin, aluminum, stainless steel wire, springs and oil paint;
   52 x 305 x 33 cm

Sculptor Lee Hyung-koo will represent Korea at the 52nd Venice Biennale, which will open this June. This will mark the first time that a single artist will occupy the entire Korean Pavilion with a solo exhibition at the biennial art exhibition in Venice. Thanks to the efforts of the late video artist Paik Nam-june (Nam June Paik), Korea became the 25th nation to have a pavilion at this event in 1995.

Lee, born in 1969, has made a name for himself by creating eerie works that resemble some kind of secret research labs for anatomical experimentation, complete with intriguing optical devices and equipment. Recently, he unveiled his "Homo Animatus" series that depicts the skeletal structures of cartoon characters, which have been described as cute and fascinating. Even people with no particular interest in modern art have been attracted to his works.

In video footage, the artist is seen nonchalantly walking along the streets of New York wearing his "optical helmet," which makes his head look four times larger than normal. Passersby giggle, while the expressions on their faces seem to say: "Hey, neat trick." Even the faces of unimpressionable urban dwellers will brighten for a

2

moment at the sight of this young artist and his black humor. It is not often that cutting-edge modern art, which deals in depth with the issues of contemporary culture, can also make people laugh.

Lee's elaborately assembled, strangely shaped skeletal works resemble fossils excavated from prehistoric strata. In response to his sculptural works, Internet users have made comments like: "Are the cartoon characters extinct?"; "The hyperrealistic detail is amazing"; and "It's cute, but also kinda creepy. It's an interesting and strange feeling." In reality, the portrayal of virtual fossils requires long hours of hard work. The artist's attitude toward the theme is no simple matter, as he inquires: "In what cultural dimensions can the human body be restructured nowadays?" And yet this scientist-like artist, with a unique charm, clearly elicits a response from the audience of his works. The following are excerpts from my interview with Lee.

LIM GEUN-JUN: The Korean Pavilion is notorious for being a difficult space for exhibitions. What are your thoughts on this?

LEE HYUNG-KOO: Everyone knows this. It is in a poor location first of all. It is small, and more than anything, the

"HK LAB-WR Performance" (2004)
Project Space Zip installation, Seoul

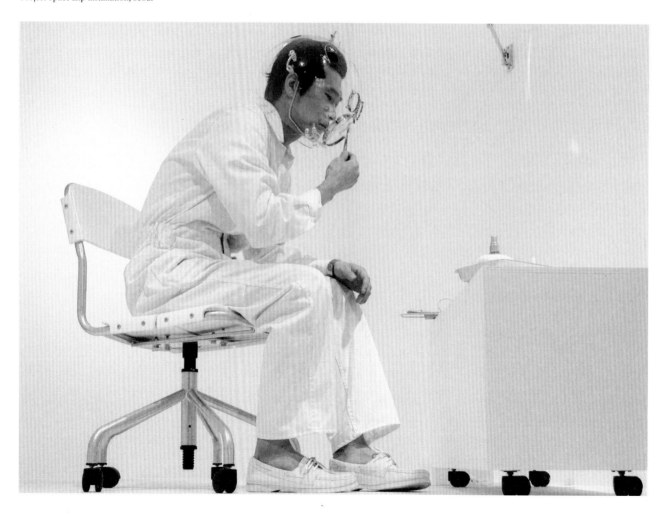

building is very inconvenient for exhibitions. (Laughter)

LIM: Which national pavilions do you like best?

LEE: The German Pavilion and the British Pavilion.

LIM: Although there has been criticism that "commissioners take pride in the fact that several artists can present exhibits in such a small pavilion," the commissioners of the Korean Pavilion have seen fit to designate a number of artists. Thus, Korea's art community was quite surprised at Commissioner Ahn So-yeon's decision to designate only one artist, which was a welcome change. When did you hear that you had been designated as the sole artist for the Korean Pavilion?

LEE: I heard unofficially in early October.

LIM: This must be a very special exhibition for both you and the commissioner.

LEE: It is. In 1997, when I was a student, I visited Venice as an assistant to a Korean Pavilion artist. Commissioner Ahn had served as the curator for the Venice Biennale Special Exhibition for Korean Contemporary Art, entitled "Tiger's Tail," which was held separately in 1995, the year when the Korean Pavilion was opened.

LIM: A second Korean Pavilion, which Mr. Paik had pushed for, has not yet become a reality, but if such a gallery space were to be established, many in the art world believe that this would come about by the hands of Curator Ahn So-yeon. There are also people who are cautiously suggesting that you might be able to return home in glory with a special prize for the Korean Pavilion.

LEE: The artist just does his best to create his works and exhibit them. Of course, it would be nice to be awarded a prize as well. (Laughter)

LIM: I have heard that you plan to display both "The Objectuals" series, consisting of optical devices that can visually and physically transform the proportions of the human body, and the "Homo Animatus" series, which portrays the skeletal structures of cartoon characters in quasi-archaeological fashion.

LEE: I plan to link the two series into one. Overall, I hope to create the atmosphere of a newly created laboratory. Particularly, I plan to stage a performance at the opening of the exhibition while wearing my "WR" optical helmet, so it will be important for me to conserve my energy so I can last to the end of the exhibition.

LIM: Oh, so will the post-human Dr. Jekyll be traveling to Venice with his laboratory?

LEE: I'm looking to open up a Venice branch. (Laughter)

LIM: How did you become involved with these kinds of projects as a student?

LEE: I have always had a keen interest in transformation based on the human body, such as mutation, physiognomy and phrenology. My research and experimentation naturally led me to this point.

LIM: When was your first performance?

LEE: My first performance was during a class in my fourth year as an undergraduate. Thereafter, I continued to present various performances. The first time that I dressed up and acted like a scientist was at an open studio of the Ssamzie Residence in 2004. Since then, I have been performing at major exhibitions.

LIM: The impression that audiences get from your performances as a scientist is not really science fiction, nor of a medical thriller, or noir. It's actually quite curious.

LEE: I joke that the core of my work is *yamae* (a term used to describe underhanded methods, often in regard to the buying or selling of items, or getting information). (Laughter)

LIM: "Yamae comes from the Japanese word *yami*, which means darkness. How many pieces have you created for the "Homo Animatus" series thus far? It takes quite a while to complete a piece, doesn't it? I've heard that you have a large number of assistants to help you.

LEE: Not counting the initial research, and beginning

1 "HK LAB-WR Performance" (2004)
   Project Space Zip installation, Seoul
2 "Altering Facial Features with Pink-H1" (2003)
   Digital print, 120 x 150 cm

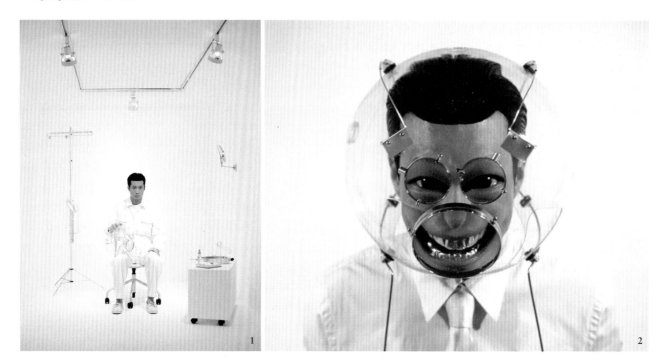

Even the faces of unimpressionable urban dwellers will brighten for a moment at the sight of this young artist and his black humor. It is not often that cutting-edge modern art, which deals in depth with the issues of contemporary culture, can also make people laugh.

with the pieces I displayed at the "2004 Youthful Seeking" exhibition at the National Museum of Contemporary Art, there would be a total of 14 pieces in nine sets. At first, it took anywhere from seven or eight months to a year to complete a single piece; so I had a tough time. I get a lot of help from assistants because the work requires a lot of attention. These days, I usually work with as many as 10, or five at least. Three assistants will be accompanying me to Venice. If it weren't for the support of the Arario Gallery, it would be incredibly difficult to work under these conditions.

LIM: Exactly what kind of material is used to make the skeletons? It looks just like bones and is quite realistic.

LEE: The material is a hard polyurethane plastic. I have been looking into using new materials these days. At first, I added some bone meal as a magical touch. (Laughter) The results didn't change, just the way I felt. There is ultimately a compromise between human bones and animal bones in an attempt to create a virtual result that may not actually exist but looks like it could. And the details make use of minute bubbles to create fine holes, so it requires a lot of work. As they say: "God is about the details."

LIM: As you make these adjustments, I imagine that there are times when you have to resort to trickery.

LEE: Of course. No matter how well a cartoon character may be planned, no one really calculates the placement of each and every bone, so ultimately there are a lot of cases in which I have to improvise. Not only do the characters change in size according to season, but sometimes they change from one scene to the next. Animators are people, too.

LIM: In particular, what features do you believe are the most absurd?

LEE: The eyeballs. They are the most exaggerated feature,

so most of the time the eyeballs and the skeleton overlap. In particular, the sockets that hold the eyeballs are joined together, causing the eyes to overlap. The most problematic feature after the eyeballs is the vertebra. In the process of transforming the cartoon characters, there are distortions, such as making the head one-third to one-fourth the size of the entire body, or four-footed creatures standing upright like humans, so the scope of change is vast.

Then, the joints for the hands and feet can be tricky. Especially when making a front foot into a hand, the joints have to be shorter, so ultimately the extent of the adjustment is greater. It is interesting that mammals have five toes on their front feet and four toes on their hind feet. But rodents generally have five toes on both their front and hind feet. At any rate, as for works of caricature, one toe or finger gets left off each limb, making for hands with four fingers and feet with three toes. And strangely enough, Jerry of "Tom & Jerry" only has two toes.

LIM: Wow, I find that so fascinating. Are you currently preparing to debut a new character after Jerry in the "Homo Animatus" series?

LEE: Not yet. Instead, I am refining the original "Homo Animatus," using the skills I have accumulated since that time. I plan to display the intermediate stages of manufacture at the Venice Biennale, and when they are completely assembled, I want to display them alongside Homo sapiens.

LIM: Wouldn't it be fantastic if you could display your series in a Victorian-style museum of natural history?

LEE: If I can get the chance, I'd like to display them at Yale University's Peabody Museum of Natural History. In truth, aren't the museums of natural history spaces all dominated by performance art?

Lim Geun-jun Art and Design Critic   **Ahn Hong-beom** Photographer

Yun Suk-nam

Installation Artist Pursues Feminist Issues

1

1 "To Be Lengthened – Water" (2002)
   Mixed media, 117 x 60 x 232 cm
2 "Kim Hye-sun" (2002)
3 "Mother 5 – For the Family" (1993)
   Acrylic on wood, 160 x 80 x 7 cm
   In this series Yun seeks a friendly relationship between
   mother and daughter.

Feminist art in Korea is generally considered to have arrived on the scene in 1986, with the group exhibition "From Half into One," featuring the works of Kim In-sun, Kim Jin-suk and Yun Suk-nam. Of these three artists, Yun Suk-nam, who has long been active in the women's movement — she is the publisher of the feminist magazine IF — is the best known for advancing the feminist perspective through her works. Yun has distinguished herself as a dedicated feminist artist with her mindset and works that have evolved naturally from her personal life experiences.

"When I began painting in 1979, the word 'feminism' was still unfamiliar in Korea. Early on, the first subject that I painted was my mother, and the mothers I saw at the marketplace. My heart felt at ease in doing so. Specifically, I wanted to understand why these women had to live such frantic lives, and why I had to live the way I did."

In Korea, "mother" is synonymous with "sacrifice." This means that, regardless of whether the concept of motherhood is a social product fabricated by a patriarchal ideology, the thought of "mother" as an eternal sanctuary that is always there to embrace you affectionately, like a warm spot nearby, is indelibly engraved in the hearts and

"Genealogy" (1993)
Mixed media, 250 x 270 x 150 cm

"When I began painting in 1979, the word 'feminism' was still unfamiliar in Korea. Early on, the first subject that I painted was my mother, and the mothers I saw at the marketplace. My heart felt at ease in doing so. Specifically, I wanted to understand why these women had to live such frantic lives, and why I had to live the way I did."

minds of all Koreans.

Yet, why is it that while various genres of art feature numerous works that depict the relationship between mother and son, there are so few that portray the mother-daughter relationship? Yun's Western-style painting series, "Mother," is a meaningful effort that seeks to demonstrate that the apparent distance between mother and daughter in Korean art is closely related to the structural contradictions of our society in regard to the status of women. Thanks to Yun's wholly committed artistic approach, greater attention is being given to such issues as the mother seen through a daughter's eyes and the kindred relationship between mother and daughter.

"In reality, if I didn't talk about my mother I couldn't have talked about myself. Like going through a rite of passage, I could not help but talk about my mother," Yun said.

To Yun, the mother's sacrifice deserves far more than a discussion of the sublime. Evidence of the patriarchal ideology that demanded sacrifice and overlooked abuse can be seen in her works. As such, the mother's sacrifice depicted in her works is characterized by a multifaceted complexity. At every corner of society there exists an excess of inhuman oppression and tragedy, such that it is not possible to rely on the concept of love and recognize sacrifice as an absolute symbol of motherhood.

The titles of the works in her "Mother" series, such as "19 Years Old," "Daughter and Son," "For the Family" and "From Within the Gate to Without," are all intended to expound on this relationship. And in each of her works, though it may appear somewhat antiquated today, her utilization of the patterns found in colorful, traditional fabrics reveal that there was a lilting poem alive in the hearts of the mothers, even when bent with age, like

Works from "To Be Lengthened" Series (2001)
Pencil and watercolor on paper, 45.5 x 30.5 cm

gnarled trees, from the weighty burdens of maintaining a family household. In particular, such a sentiment is a reflection of the inner side of a mother, which could only be perceived by a daughter.

After reaching the age of motherhood, a daughter who reflects upon her mother comes to better understand the depth of her trials and bitter life experiences. Of course, these mothers were nevertheless high-spirited and in good health in order to dutifully look after their family.

Yun says, "I like going to the traditional market, where the coarse and boisterous voices, laughter and bantering were brimming with vitality. What I feel from these mothers is not so much sadness, but rather their perseverance." Her art career, which started out with the subject of mothers, continued on with such series as "Pink Room," "The Seeding of Lights" and "To Be Lengthened." In terms of style and media, her initial "Mother" series was comprised of two-dimensional paintings, but she later created installation works made from wood, which has since

become her trademark medium. As for Yun's love for working with wood, is this somehow related to her feminist advocacy?

Yun recalled: "In the early 1990s, I visited the birthplace of Heo Nanseolheon [a woman poet of the 16th-century Joseon period] in Gangneung, where there was a grove filled with persimmon trees. I picked up a fallen branch and carved the poet's name onto it. As I handled the wood, it felt like the skin of a woman. The wood was warm, with a soothing and wrinkled grain — just like the skin of an old woman. If you drew a face on that wood it would become a woman."

Born in Shenyang (formerly Fengtian), Manchuria, in 1939, Yun was introduced to painting during her days at Seoul National University Middle School. At the age of 40, in 1979, she embarked on her career as a painter. In 1983, she went to the United States for a year to study woodblock printing. Her diligent work ethic allowed her not only to overcome her handicap as a latecomer, but to

그녀가 왜 저위에 앉아 있는지, 어떻게 올라 갔는지, 왜 아니 내려 오는지 우리는 알지 못한다.
그녀가 저 위에 처음 한 후 한동안 그녀를 걱정했던 사람들이 모두 다 바쁘기 때문이다. 나만 아직 여기에서 기다리고 있다.
이제는 모두 그녀를 잊어 버렸다. 그 위에서 무엇을 보았는지 알고 싶기 때문이다. 2002. 3. 11. 윤원석남

1 "Pink Room 3" (1996)
Mixed media
This work portrays the uneasy and precarious life of Korean women today.
2 "Blue Bell" (2002)
Mixed media, H. 187 cm.

attain notable success, leading to her first solo exhibition in 1992. She has also actively participated in exhibitions that dealt with women-related themes and issues, including "Women and Reality," "Women, Their Differences and Strengths" and the "Women's Art Festival: Patjwis on Parade."

Despite the late start in her art career, in just a brief time Yun emerged as a talented artist worthy of attention. This indicates that just as her feminist perspective is rooted in some innate quality, the same is true of her profound love for and devotion to art. As was the case with van Gogh and Gauguin, it seemed to be part of Yun's destiny to ultimately engage in artistic pursuits at some point in her life. In the mid-1990s, she was able to move beyond talking about her mother and to talk about herself through her "Pink Room" series. She had this to say about the series: "When I finished working on 'Mother,' I felt as if I had completed a lengthy shaman ritual. Then I gained the courage to talk about myself. 'Pink Room'

is about me. It could be called the story of the mothers around me. I wanted to portray my place, and the place of mothers. Actually, I have only recently had my own room. When describing my place in life, I instinctively talk about 'Pink Room.' What I present in 'Pink Room' is a Western-style chair, onto which I place Korean clothing, creating an awkward juxtaposition of two cultures. It was as if this symbolized the uneasy place of women, who cannot be in either the kitchen or their room."

Her "Pink Room" series consists of installation works that feature such items as Western furniture, a large nail and pink beads. They depict the reality of unease and uncertainty imposed upon middle-class women in Korea today, beleaguered by the omnipotence of materialism, dissolution of the family and a loss of identity. Yun yearns for women to overcome this age of crisis through their resolute solidarity. This desire is expressed in "The Seeding of Light" series, which features 999 trees, and the more recent "To Be Lengthened" series. "I want to touch

someone, to reach out and place my arm around another's shoulder," she says. "Yet in real life, a woman cannot reach out to other women. This may also be related to the inherent loneliness of people. Women in particular want to reach out to each other, and after having made such contact, to then realize some accomplishment. Is there not much that we cannot accomplish?"

Yun tries to reach out to others in part because she hopes to overcome the basic loneliness of humanity, and also because she desires to have women, as opposed to being outsiders on the fringes, move toward the center with a kindred spirit. The woman in her 2003 work, "To Be Lengthened," extends her hand as an expression of this spirit. By stretching out her hand she is extending herself. What makes this work memorable, though, is that the hand this woman is extending is separated from her wrist.

Consequently, a viewer's attention is naturally focused on the matter of whether her hand can somehow be reconnected with her wrist, rather than wondering if her

hand will reach whatever it is trying to touch. The task for this woman is to first regain her hand. It is meaningful to note that the work leaves the viewer with an impression that this situation does not involve any specific woman, but symbolizes the reality that all women encounter. In this way, the woman who seeks to reach out with her hand can find herself faced with seemingly insurmountable obstacles from the very start. But in the end, this is no more than a catalyst for the eventual advancement of modern society.

If women can take that first step toward genuine love and solidarity, we can move toward a world of greater compassion, peace and fulfillment. Until that time, the installation art of Yun will continue along its path of boundless expansion. In this regard, the poet Kim Hye-sun has eloquently observed: "In the works of Yun Suk-nam, the road ahead flows from the eyes and hands."

Yi Joo-heon Art Critic **Choi Hang-young** Photographer

Bae Bien-u

Zooming into the Soul of Korean Landscapes

From "Pine Trees" Series
Bae Bien-u believes the images of pine trees best reflect the
fundamental character of the Korean people.

If you drive along the California coast beyond the town of Carmel, you will come to Point Lobos, where fantastic rock formations combine with majestic pines to create a scene of overwhelming grandeur. The local Native Americans of old are said to have regarded this landscape as being so sacred that they would not disturb a tree or a rock, or obstruct the natural flow of seawater or passage of the wind. It seems that this is why Point Lobos has managed to retain its original appearance throughout the centuries. It was this natural splendor of Point Lobos that helped to produce a true master of photography, Edward Weston. Weston would be ranked, along with another renowned landscape photographer, Ansel Adams, as the most American of photographers. In particular, these two share an inimitable ability to infuse the magnificent light of nature, and its spectacular forms, with an American soul and spirit.

Nature, and its underlying soul and spirit, are essential to a landscape photographer because without soul a landscape scene becomes trivial, and without spirit, it becomes barren. Therefore, to a landscape photographer, the existence of soul and spirit in nature is all-important. Among Korean photographers, who then could be said to possess a purity of soul and spirit comparable to that of Edward Weston? To this question, the first name that springs to mind may well be Bae Bien-u, who has come to be recognized as Korea's quintessential landscape photographer.

Bae, who has long been photographing Korean landscapes, expresses the Korean sentiments for everyone to see in his distinctive black-and-white images. Indeed, it could be said that Bae and his works are synonymous with Korea's contemporary photography. Through Korean landscapes, he has discovered a Korean aesthetic, which he has sought to imbue with universal sensibilities. His photographs are suffused with the purity and integrity of

Bae's photographs define his critical aesthetic and artistic evaluation. His fantasy-like panoramic images are capable of stirring delicate sensations and arresting the eyes and heart, while causing viewers to encounter a soul and spirit beyond conventional beauty through uniquely natural lines, forms, and tones.

traditional ink paintings. He focuses first and foremost on the lyrical essence of a landscape scene. Then, he seeks to highlight the soul and spirit therein. Each of his series has been undertaken from this approach: "Marado," "Pine Trees," "Jeju Sea," "Parasite Cones" (secondary volcanic cones found scattered about Jeju Island), and "Hyangi-ram Cliff." From the time he first developed an interest in photography, Bae has been enchanted by landscapes. To this day, he has never strayed from landscapes for even an instant. His attention has thus remained intently focused on nature as he strives to capture nature's unpretentious-ness in black and white, as if creating an ink painting.

"The oldest picture in my memory is a crayon draw-ing, which was hung on the back wall of the classroom when I was in the second grade of elementary school. It showed a low tiled house crouching under a big tree on a hill, with the sea visible in the background. I seem to have lived my whole life with this image stuck in my mind. It may even have been this image that influenced my inter-est in such subjects as the sea, pine trees, rock formations and parasite cones. From the time when I attended an art college, I have wandered around the islands off the south coast with an old Nikon-F and a Mamiya double-lens. Although I can't say that all the photographs I've taken to this day have been images of Korean things and the Korean soul and spirit, I have never thought of my pho-tographs as anything different from that picture from my second grade classroom in elementary school, which to me was a landscape of Korea as well as my heart."

Bae knows well how to capture the unadorned ele-

From "Hyangiram Cliff" Series
Throughout his career, Bae has consistently sought to depict the transparency of nature with his black-and-white landscape photography.

gance of Korean landscapes. Whether in black and white or in color, he creates wonderful images that express a Korean sensibility. In reaching this point of his career, he has learned much from others. In particular, Bae has gained valuable insight from such masters as Laszlo Moholy-Nagy and Edward Weston. From Moholy-Nagy, he acquired a new concept of light, and from Weston a new approach to nature. Adding to this were the pine trees that he encountered while trekking along the Tae-baek Mountain Range, which forms the backbone of the Korean peninsula. It was through the pines that he eventually discovered the grandeur of light, the paramount aspect of landscapes, and the transcendence of Korean lines.

Bae said: "Suddenly, in the lines of pine trees, I saw an image of absolute spirituality and soulfulness. From their distorted forms, it dawned on me that this was an ideal symbol of the Korean sentiments. These lines of the soul and spirit expanded to become the horizontal lines of the Jeju Sea, the curved lines of Jeju parasite cones, and the vertical lines of Hyangiram Cliff. Neither big nor small, neither jagged nor smooth, one might call them moderate lines. Through the lines of Korean landscapes I wanted to express a uniquely Korean aesthetic."

Bae expresses himself through lines. He presents a world of lines in harmony with light, which extends beyond traditional beauty to a realm of the soul and spirit. The pines of Gyeongju thus serve as a representative standard of Korean lines. The upright, firm lines reflect the dignified propriety and resoluteness of the Korean people,

1 "The Soul Garden – Alhambra"
2 "The Soul Garden – Changdeok Palace"

while the extended, graceful lines symbolize their resilience amid a turbulent history. In the lines of pine trees, Bae found the epitome of the Korean character and the fateful plight of a tenacious and robust people. As a result, lines are a recurring motif in his photographs and an aesthetic framework to illuminate the spirit and soul as well as the self.

At the same time, the aesthetic of lines is of a universal nature as well. No matter what subject he photographs, the lines of the image reveal his personal aesthetic and universal character. Through his photographic interpretation, Bae can highlight both the Korean and universal sensibility of any subject. A representative example of this is his "Tahiti" series. The landscape scenery of Tahiti is indeed exotic, but it takes on a Korean and universal aesthetic in

Bae's photographs. His Tahiti photographs demonstrate that place is no longer an issue. As such, based on the view, distance, and attitude adopted toward a subject, the photographs of any country or landscape can feature the photographer's lines, tones, and sentiments.

Of particular note, Bae's photographs define his critical aesthetic and artistic evaluation. His fantasy-like panoramic images are capable of stirring delicate sensations and arresting the eyes and heart, while causing viewers to encounter a soul and spirit beyond conventional beauty through uniquely natural lines, forms, and tones. He presents a profound essence of nature, with a universal appeal, through his transcendent lines and forms.

Jin Dong-sun Photography Critic

Koo Bohn-chang
Images Reflect the Other Side of Life

Photographer Koo Bohn-chang's "Masks" series is currently being exhibited at the Hanmi Gallery in Seoul. Long concerned with both the visible and the invisible aspects of life, Koo has addressed various issues of life through the images of masks. For the past 20 years, he has approached society by way of the self, and through society he has dealt with matters of existence and non-existence. The relationships among these elements can be found throughout his oeuvre, serving as codes to reflect the duality of self and non-self, nature and mankind, body and mind, and creation and extinction.

Koo Bohn-chang's 1988 work, "Clandestine Pursuit in the Long Afternoon," focuses on the intersection between the self and the totality, where we encounter ourselves through others and reaffirm others through ourselves. For Koo, a photograph is a reflection of the self, while the view of its subject is at the same time a mirror and a window on the fleeting meanings that recede into the world. From this point of view, "Clandestine Pursuit in the Long Afternoon" presents a momentary glimpse of the end of the world as seen by an anonymous stranger. A stranger who was not so much a stranger, an outsider who lived on the outskirts of life and felt alienated — this was the sense

2

captured by the camera. The point where the self and non-self intersect, when the view of the subject becomes that of an observer maintaining a certain distance, a wounded spirit who circles over Seoul in search of freedom dreams of escaping from his fettered existence.

Koo said, "When I returned to Seoul after spending six years studying in Germany, everything seemed so unfamiliar. The freedom I had enjoyed in Germany was suddenly restricted, and I suffered. 'Clandestine Pursuit in the Long Afternoon' was my quest to escape this suffering and rediscover my free self."

The freedom of the automatic camera reveals where this "stalking" ends. The scenes of life "captured" by the automatic camera were specifically the scenes of feeling left out, refracted through the lives of others. They showed the elements of life that could not be spoken of, which

were too minute to be visible in the world. All the more unfamiliar due to their triviality, these were the images of Koo striving to cope with life in Seoul. The automatic camera was the medium that could immediately illuminate, capture and reveal these aspects. The ambiguity of truth and falsehood, the meaning of living in this land, the incongruity of the coexistence of dissimilarities — through juxtaposition of the exposed and the hidden natures of such relationships, Koo sought to convey contemporary life and scenes of anomie.

In "Goodbye Paradise" (1993), Koo was concerned less with points of contact between the self and the whole than with the homogeneity of all living things. He sought to demonstrate that even the most minuscule insect or the most ordinary creature is essentially no different from a human being. Believing that all living things possess a

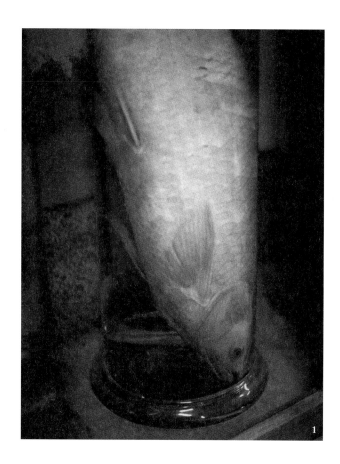

soul, he endeavored to portray these muted spirits through the images of insects on display at a natural history museum, where these dead and stuffed souls speak with silent voices.

Mounted butterflies and insect specimens were the insignificant, and therefore unheard, things with which Koo attempted to listen, inquire, and converse. Listening to these souls took on a new form through the sound of his father's breathing. "Breath" (1995) was a tale of death that sought to depict the reality about human life and existence. The artist's father in the photographs is also Koo's alter ego, not just as a father, but at the same time as another universal human image standing at the boundary separating life and death. But it was no easy matter to expose such things. In the artist's words: "I had great qualms about photographing my dying father. I wanted to say that 'Breath' was how life looked in its last moments, when any human faces death. But because the subject was my father, my other family members couldn't understand me, and I must admit that their feelings seemed natural to me, too."

And so, in the image of his dying father, Koo portrayed the reality of human death. He wanted to experience what it meant for humans to breathe at the threshold of existence and non-existence. With the "In the Beginning"

series of 1995, he featured the self as the measure of existence in a more radical manner. "In the Beginning," which addresses the significance of the body and its existential identity, arose from Koo's realization that his father's death and his father's body lay at the root of his own identity, inseparable from himself.

Koo perceives the human body as an existential form that arises at birth from the bond with, and separation from, another person's body. To express this perception, he has connected, stitched, and sewn together images of bodies with needle and thread in the darkroom. These connected bodies appear as if wounded by the abrasions of life and its fleeting temporality.

Koo explained: "At first, I just wanted to enlarge the body. But I couldn't express myself that way, due to practical physical constraints. Since no print paper was large enough, I had to attach sheets of paper together to create larger forms, and in the process, I came to see the meaning of the human body in a new light. Stitching pieces of print paper together in the darkroom, I saw the needle marks on those attractive bodies, and the image of the thread like a suture stitching up a wound. Suddenly, the body conveyed a kind of connection or combination by means of the needle and thread."

In the process of attaching together sheets of print

"Masks (GA 03), Five Clowns of Gasan" (2002)
Gelatin silver print

paper with a sewing machine or by hand-stitching, Koo saw how lives that had become fragmented or worn out like rags could be renewed when joined together. And he felt this was one of time's traces that human beings inevitably bear during their lifetime.

With the opening of the new millennium, Koo also entered a new world of ideas. This included his "White" series, consisting of photographs that were entirely white. In photography, white is used to symbolize death and extinction. Just as gray hair symbolizes aging and skeletal bones death, white is used to depict aging and dying. An absence of color foretells death. The ivy growing on the white walls stands out as a representation of life and death. Thus, Koo's photographic art had expanded in concept to include the issues of life and death expressed through natural subjects.

"I wondered what it would be like if the print paper turned white. White is the look of black that has faded, of color that has been drained away. Through the subject of ivy growing on white walls, I contemplated matters related to life and death," Koo said. In approaching the issues of death and extinction through color, in using natural rather than artificial subjects, and in expressing himself so directly, Koo marked a clear departure from his earlier work.

The unceasing flow of time eventually brought him into contact with yet another world, where he encountered the masks. It was an entirely unexpected meeting. But through masks he again explored the theme of life and its hidden elements. Masks rekindled the flames of the artist's desire to move between the extremes of existence and non-existence. A mask is a tool that can hide the truth and project feelings through facial expressions alone. Someone wearing a mask is a mediator between concealment and revelation of true feelings, or a messenger of communica-

tion between the self and others.

Koo has these observations about masks: "While taking these pictures, it suddenly occurred to me that the character within the mask could be me. There were times when I wondered whether the mask was an image of myself living my lonely life, or whether the emotions expressed in the masks were those of my own circumstances as I lived my life."

The masked figures in his photographs face straight forward in a rigid pose. The stiff bodies behind the affixed masks stand motionless as if frozen. Perhaps because the photographer sees himself in these subjects, the images in the pictures are frozen in fettered forms.

An artist who contemplates profoundly about self and whole, life and death, Koo has spent the past 20 years telling of things that do not appear readily on the surface. "From Clandestine Pursuit in the Long Afternoon" (1988) to "Masks" (2003), he has devoted his career to portraying things that cannot be told, of things that vanish into the shadows of existence. This is why life and death, existence and non-existence, are the essence of his photographs. And mediating between these worlds, time and memory have formed a backdrop for his realm of imagery. As a result, Koo's world of photography resides in a domain that cannot be placed neatly within a frame.

The photographs that Koo has produced since returning from his studies in Germany are like a diary of real life. They are also an intriguing gateway into the unknown. With warm blood pulsing through the far and the near side of life for all five senses, Koo's photographs are both an expression of life and a silent cry on behalf of beings without a voice.

Jin Dong-sun Photo Critic

Stage Artists

Lee Ae-joo
Master Dancer with Social Awareness

Acropolis Plaza of Seoul National University on June 29, 1987. Students had been steadily gathering since noon to participate in a ceremony to start the "June 29 Peace March." It had been whispered around that certain professors helped to organize an anti-government dance performance to support the students. Indeed, with anticipation, the atmosphere on the plaza couldn't have been more tense. Then, a petite, yet charismatic, woman appeared on the stage and began to dance.

The opening act was "The Seed," an introduction to life; the second and third acts were "Water" and "Fire," respectively, portraying a fierce clash between the ruthless forces of death and the grassroots populace. The final act was "The Flower of Hope," an appeal for resurrection. The entire solo piece, entitled "Dance for Greeting the Wind" (*Baram maji chumpan*), was performed by Professor Lee Ae-joo.

Lee recalls that day: "The brisk footsteps of the students coming to take part in the Peace March and the fluttering flags were like the blaring of horns to warn of an enemy advance. This energized me. As I prepared to take my first steps, I could hardly believe my body's movement. When I thrust my bare foot into the air toward

the sky, my whole body seemed to float upward. It was a free, spontaneous movement. I just danced and danced my heart out. When I finished, the students cheered and shouted, and then poured out onto the streets. When I saw my picture in the newspapers the next day, I was astonished. I had never seen such a dance photo, or rather, such a dance movement. My body arching toward the sky, fists clenched tight, legs jumping freely, coordinated movement of hands and feet — all defining features of Korean dance, forming an outline of the Korean peninsula. My body was portraying the shape of my country."

This photograph of Lee was published by the foreign press; it was a historic image that aroused interest around the world about the pro-democracy movement in Korea. Her photograph helped to move Korea's democracy one step forward.

The struggle for democracy had been ignited when Seoul National University student Park Jong-cheol died on January 14, 1987, after being beaten and tortured during a police interrogation. Anti-government protests further intensified on June 9 that year when Yonsei University student Lee Han-yeol was killed after being struck by a tear-gas canister thrown by riot police to quell a

demonstration staged by some 1,000 students in front of his university. Thereafter, a crowd of one million citizens gathered in front of the Seoul City Hall; Lee Ae-joo was leading the rally.

What is the source of Lee's boundless energy? First, it would be helpful to review her lengthy dance career.

Born in 1947 in Bongsan, Hwanghae-do Province, now in North Korea, Lee began to learn dance at the age of seven. While studying under Kim Bo-nam (1911–1964) at the National Traditional Music Institute, predecessor of the National Center for Korean Traditional Performing Arts, Lee met Han Yeong-suk (1920–1989) in 1969, whose instruction enabled her to master *seungmu*, the Buddhist monk's dance. Han was the granddaughter of Han Seong-jun (1875–1941), a *pansori* master who played a key role in refining traditional Korean dances and songs into performing arts.

Most people think of seungmu as a dance performed by Buddhist monks at temple ceremonies, but this is not

entirely true. It was also a solo dance performed at secular banquets and festivals by a dancer wearing a monk's flowing white robe with long extended sleeves, a red sash and a white conical headpiece. While rooted in Buddhist dance as well as folk arts such as mask dance and farmers' music, it was developed into a highly refined solo dance. Thanks in large part to the efforts of Han Seong-jun, the monk's dance was performed at public venues during the final years of the Joseon period (1392–1910). The dance has a variety of regional versions, of which the first to be designated an "important intangible cultural property" was the version rooted in Gyeonggi and Chungcheong provinces and refined by Han Seong-jun. His student and granddaughter, Han Yeong-suk, was named a "human treasure," or a master performer, of the monk's dance. With her death, the title was passed on to Lee in 1996.

Seungmu begins slowly and mysteriously with almost imperceptible movements. Then, the dancer throws her long sleeves to draw big waves in the air and beats the drum to a fast six-beat rhythm before dancing in gracefully flowing movements. She draws her hands from the sleeves to beat the drum, first slowly, then gathering speed, building up to a crescendo, and finally returning to a four-count beat, until her sleeves are dramatically unfurled to mark the finale.

Lee has been designated a "human treasure," affirming her brilliant artistry in the highly intricate classical dance style. But just as importantly, Lee's dance is intertwined with her desire to alleviate the oppressiveness of society. Therefore, after graduating from the Department of Physical Education at Seoul National University, she enrolled in the Department of Korean Language and Literature at the same university the following year. Her original purpose was to study dance from a more academic perspective, but this department was also where leaders of the student movement for democracy gathered. Among them were Kim Ji-ha, Chae Hee-wan, Kim Min-gi and Lim Chintack (who later became Lee's brother-in-law). Lee taught

Korean dance to this group, who taught her about the basic principles of *minjung* (people's) ideology.

Lee also passionately sought to perfect the techniques and spirit of *salpurichum* (exorcist dance), which Han Seong-jun had also refined. A dance to console the souls of the deceased and comfort the living, salpurichum is highly improvisational. As such, it undergoes constant change according to time and place, while seeking to heighten the audience's consciousness of their existence. In 1974, Lee presented her version of the dance, a result of her dedicated efforts over years.

Because of her political activism, Lee was under constant surveillance by the military government, which led her to leave for the United States in 1978. During her four years in New York, she did odd jobs, such as working at a supermarket and selling small goods on the streets. But she maintained her desire to learn and enrolled in a Ph.D. program at New York University, and even studied modern dance under Martha Graham.

Lee Ae-joo performs "Dance for Greeting the Wind" at the Seoul National University campus on June 29, 1987.

Lee has been designated a "human treasure," affirming her brilliant artistry in the highly intricate classical dance style. But just as importantly, Lee's dance is intertwined with her desire to alleviate the oppressiveness of society.

"From Martha Graham's work 'Release and Contraction,' I found that the breathing method that Western dancers used was actually an Asian technique," Lee noted. "Once I realized this, I thought that rather than learning what I already know from someone else, through a different technique, it would be better to further improve my dance. I started teaching seungmu to Korean students and some Americans as well, when I was offered a professorship at Seoul National University. So, I returned home in 1982."

It was surprising that Lee received such an offer from the conservative state university, especially under the government of Chun Doo-hwan, who succeeded the military dictatorship of Park Chung-hee. Undoubtedly, this was proof of the high acclaim she was enjoying for her mastery of Korean dance. While diligently teaching her students, she joined a movement to promote Korean folk culture. This led to her performances of "*Nanum gut*" (Exorcism of Sharing), which called for social justice, and "*Dorajik-kot*" (Bellflowers), which depicted the suffering of "comfort women," who were forced by imperial Japan to serve as sex slaves for its troops during World War II. Eventually, in 1987, her presentation of "*Baram maji chumpan*" (Dance for Greeting the Wind) marked the culmination of this process.

"In the 'Dance for Greeting the Wind,' the wind, or *baram*, has a dual meaning. It refers to resistance in the face of a destructive wind that can wreak havoc, and rallying behind a rousing wind with the power to revive the oppressed and even the dead," Lee explained.

While immersing herself in a search for ways to express these sentiments, Lee would burn with passion at times and also weep for those who suffer injustice. In 1987, when Lee accepted a position with the Minjung Party, which named Paik Ki-wan as its candidate for the presidential election, she came under fire as many speculated about her political ambition. But with her small progressive party having little hope of winning the election, Lee's actions could be interpreted as a symbolic protest against the authoritarian regime of that time.

For sometime thereafter, Lee seemed to fade out of the public's sight. However, this did not mean she had stopped dancing. She performed at an international conference in Japan in 1988, which called for the elimination of nuclear weapons; the Asian Folk Festival in 1995; and the first World Folk Festival, held in the Netherlands in 1996. Every year since the 1990s, she has presented a memorial dance recital in honor of her teacher, Han Yeong-suk, while participating in other performances as well. All the while she has been searching for the origin of Korean dance, which she believes she has finally discovered in the ancient Korean tradition of "*yeongga mudo*," or singing and dancing.

"It includes chanting, singing, dancing and jumping, which strives to attain a state in which heaven, earth and man can become one," Lee said. "Only when humanity and nature are in harmony can the laws of nature be clearly revealed in the sounds and movements of human beings. Though there are no artificial rules for singing and dancing, there is a certain order and method, such as the five basic sounds: *eum*, *ah*, *eo*, *i* and *u*. These sounds correspond to the five major organs of the human body, and when they are strung together like beads, and raised and lowered, or bent and straightened, they become a song."

Dance is a natural movement of the body to the rhythm of song. As such, if the sounds are lengthy, the body slumps, but when the sounds pick up speed, to form phrases of a rhythm, the body becomes animated, stepping around and making movements. As the dance quickens, when the bodily movement and music reach a peak, the performer collapses onto the floor, while a soothing melody signals a return to the beginning. And in this way,

Lee performs "Dance of Life" at Cheomseongdan, the "Star Gazing Altar," on Mt. Mani in May 1991.

the body and mind are cleansed and revitalized. Accordingly, Lee thinks of yeongga mudo as a form of meditation. In April 2005, I accompanied Lee on a tour of six major universities in the United States to present lectures on Korean culture and dance demonstrations. At each session, the audience showed a keen interest in yeongga mudo and salpuri.

In February last year, Lee staged an event, entitled "Lee Ae-joo's Dance and Stories," at the University of California at Berkeley, under the sponsorship of the university's Center for Korean Studies. Based on the theme of "Korean Traditional Dance: Penetrating 10,000 Years of History with Movement of the Soul," the goal of the performance

was to demonstrate the "nothingness" of dance, featuring the movements of an ascetic integrating the mind, body and breath to attain a state of enlightenment. She started with yeongga mudo, and with elegant movements laid the groundwork for a ritual dance, sword dance, salpuri, *taepyeongmu* (dance of peace), seungmu, and finally *barachum* (cymbal dance). Thus she delivered the results of her research into the murals in the Tomb of Dancers (Muyongchong) of the Goguryeo period (37 B.C.–A.D. 668).

Kim Moon-hwan Professor of Aesthetics, Seoul National University
Lee Eun-joo Photographer

Kang Sue-jin (Sue Jin Kang)
Prima Ballerina Dazzles Global Audiences

Her feet, covered with scars and calluses, the toes twisted and nails chipped and broken, are painful to look at. At a glance, they almost look like gnarled tree roots. These misshapen feet, described as "the most beautiful feet in the world," belong to the world-class ballerina Kang Sue-jin (Sue Jin Kang). They are a testament to her dedication to a rigorous training routine of more than 10 hours a day, wearing out more than 250 pairs of toe shoes in a year. The renowned Korean poet Ko Un once said: "When I saw a picture of her feet, my heart beat so hard that I had to calm myself down, my hand pressed to my chest. I was truly moved."

On July 7, 2007, the Stuttgart Ballet staged a special performance of "Romeo and Juliet," an especially popular work among German audiences. At the end of the performance, as the prima ballerina Kang Sue-jin who played the role of Juliet appeared on stage for a curtain call, the capacity audience of about 1,500 people gave her a wild standing ovation. A banner with her name was unfurled and each of the 70 members of the Stuttgart Ballet presented a rose to her. The theater again reverberated with enthusiastic cheers and applause.

The performance was a special tribute to Kang marking her 20th year with the German ballet company. She is currently a permanent member and principal dancer of the Stuttgart Ballet, which she joined in 1986 at the age of 19, as the youngest newcomer in the company's 400-year history. It was indeed a rarity for a world-class ballet group, with time-honored traditions, to present a special tribute for an active member. Earlier in the year in March, Kang was bestowed the honorary title Kammertänzerin (German for "Royal Court Dancer"), one of only four dancers to have been so honored by the Stuttgart Ballet over the past 50 years.

Then, in September 2007, she received the John Cranko Award, named after the legendary choreographer John Cranko (1927–1973), who brought global fame to the Stuttgart Ballet with his preeminent creative artistry. The award is presented to individuals whose excellence in dance is evaluated to best represent the lofty standards of John Cranko. Announcing its selection of Kang, the Stuttgart Ballet stated: "We respectfully honor Sue Jin Kang for her unique interpretation and excellent artistry in performing John Cranko's representative works." The statement confirmed her standing as one of the most outstanding performers of Cranko's works.

The shining aura of Kang's storybook career, however, has not been without its own twists and turns. In fact, she's been walking a lonely path, while embracing her daily pain as "a normal routine" and devoting herself to severe training that eventually produced her "beautiful feet."

In 1979, when she was a seventh grader at Sunhwa Arts Middle School in Seoul, Kang had her first, fateful encounter with the world of ballet. One day during class, her teacher asked if any of the students wanted to learn ballet. Kang raised her hand. Until that time, she had been learning traditional Korean dance. In traditional Korean dance, the dancers usually turn their feet inward while in ballet, the dancers turn their feet mostly outward. Kang thus had to realign her feet through endless practice. Then, after a year and a half of training in ballet, she captured first place in a competition organized by Ewha Womans University. In 1982, she went to study at the Princess Grace Academy of Classical Dance (Académie de Danse Classique) in Monte Carlo, Monaco, after principal dancer Marika Besobrasova's visit to Sunhwa Arts

Kang Sue-jin, a principal dancer of the Stuttgart Ballet, performs in "The Taming of the Shrew."

"When I wake up in the morning, I always feel certain pain. If I don't feel any pain, I would think: 'Gee, I guess I didn't practice enough.' If you perform ballet, you feel pain all the time, so I have tried to make friends with pain. Suffering is normal for me."

High School, where she took notice of Kang's talent and potential and invited her to attend the academy for specialized training. Kang was 15 years old.

The academy's dormitory strictly enforced a lights-out regulation at 9:00 every night. Kang waited until 11 o'clock, after the security guards completed their rounds, then sneaked into an upstairs studio to practice late into the night by the moonlight filtering in through the windows or light from the adjacent palace. She felt she needed to keep up with the other students who were far more accomplished. In 1985, shortly before her graduation, she became the first Asian performer to win the Prix de Lausanne. The following year, she knocked on the door of the Stuttgart Ballet in the hope of learning classical and neo-classical ballet as well as modern ballet at the same time. That was how the "Steel Butterfly" legend began.

On her way to join the ranks of the world's elite ballerinas, Kang had to become accustomed to chronic pain.

"When I wake up in the morning, I always feel certain pain. If I don't feel any pain, I would think, 'Gee, I guess I didn't practice enough.' If you perform ballet, you feel pain all the time, so I have tried to make friends with pain. For me suffering is absolutely normal."

In 2000, Kang experienced a serious setback when she fractured an ankle bone and was consequently sidelined for a year. She had attempted to return to practice despite excruciating pain, forcing her doctor to prescribe a "temporary stay away from dancing." While worrying about whether she could ever dance again, she fell into a state of crisis, but Reid Anderson, artistic director of the company, called her one day and promised her: "Sue Jin, don't worry. We'll wait for your recovery no matter how much time it takes." Encouraged as well by her colleague Tunchi Shockman, who told her, "You can make it back," she gritted her teeth and doubled her resolve. Indeed, Kang "loved dancing far too much to give up," and by

1 "Legend" performed at the Seongnam Dance Festival 2009.
2 "Grand pas Classic" performed at the LG Arts Center in July 2007.

2002, she had overcome her injury and made a return to the stage. She also became a permanent member of the Stuttgart Ballet and married Tunchi Shockman.

What does ballet mean to Kang? "It's my life. I can't imagine my life without ballet," she said. "That has not changed ever since I joined the Stuttgart Ballet 24 years ago. Most of all, it's so important to practice everyday and perform whenever possible. I think talent makes up only one percent and the rest is from perspiration." She repeatedly emphasized: "To become a great ballerina, you need to have talent and the body for it, but without constant training and great patience, you can never achieve your goal."

Even today, she is up by six every morning and practices for six to eight hours daily when not preparing for a scheduled performance. During her early years, she practiced for up to 19 hours a day for an upcoming performance. Back then, she often ran through three or four pairs of toe shoes in a single day, whereas most other dancers used up only a single pair over two weeks or even

longer. This even caused the equipment manager to tell her she was greatly exceeding her "shoes allowance."

Apart from wearing out countless pairs of toe shoes, Kang's rigorous training regime took a serious physical toll on her, deforming her feet and constantly causing blisters leading to inflammation that never fully healed. She once had to stuff uncooked meat into her shoes for padding because her toes were so raw. "During performances, blood sometimes seeped through, but there was nothing else I could do," she recalls. The knotty calluses on every joint of her toes, however, have served as an immutable foundation upon which her stellar career has been built.

Dance critic Jang Kwang-ryul has said that "sometimes male dancers are reluctant to perform with Kang, because once, after a practice session with her, a male performer ended up being completely exhausted and dehydrated." Jang went on to remark: "But that's Kang Suejin. After pushing herself to such extremes in practice, she can be flawless on stage, gliding about so effortlessly, as if defying gravity."

Kang is known for her captivating artistry and creative expression overwhelming her audiences. Jang, who has followed Kang throughout her career, believes that her star power is a result of her "exquisite technical mastery based on ceaseless training and an ability to bring characters to life with her own interpretation and style."

Over the past 20 years, Kang has performed lead roles in over 20 ballets, including "The Sleeping Beauty," "The Magic Flute" and "Romeo and Juliet," in addition to being cast in various roles in more than 80 other productions. Many of these works featured demanding scenes created by world-renowned choreographers, such as John Cranko, Maurice Béjart, Jirí Kylián, John Neumeier, William Forsythe, Hans van Manen, Christopher Wheeldon, Nacho Duato, and Renato Zanella. All this while, she has consistently earned high praise from critics and audiences.

In "The Lady of the Camellias," Kang performed the role of the high-class prostitute Margaret, who yearns for an impossible love, which she presented with her ingenious interpretation. Then, in "Onegin," she gracefully portrayed an entirely different kind of character in Tatiana, an earnest and compassionate woman. In "Romeo and Juliet," she performed the youthful Juliet to perfection though she was over 40, earning rave reviews from critics. She noted: "Whatever your age, you can appear to be seventeen or seventy if you wholly immerse yourself into the role."

At the Seongnam Dance Festival 2009, she again revealed her passion for ballet, saying: "As long as my body allows me to do what I want, I will continue to dance." In June, she was part of a "Romeo and Juliet" performance tour of Spain, and also performed in "Onegin" in Stuttgart. At an age when most ballerinas have long bid farewell to the stage, Kang remains at the peak of her career. "The past and the future are not important. It is important to practice and to live for today. I intend to focus all my energy on how I can improve and perform even better than yesterday," she said.

Chung Sang-young Reporter, The Hankyoreh
Jung Hyung-woo Photographer

James Jeon

Broadening the Horizons of Ballet

James Jeon is a revered figure in the Korean dance world, in which original ballet works have been few and far between. The Seoul Ballet Theater, led by Jeon and his wife Kim In-hui, is noteworthy as well, since the list of professional ballet companies in Korea has previously included only the National Ballet Company, the Universal Ballet and the Gwangju Municipal Dance Company. To properly evaluate the significance of Jeon and his company, it is necessary to understand Korea's overall dance environment.

Dance in Korea, other than traditional and folk dance, can be grouped for convenience into three categories: Korean dance, contemporary dance, and ballet. Students generally major in one of these areas before going on to join a professional company and then working as a dancer or a choreographer based on their inclination and ability. Although there is no shortage of creative choreographers in the fields of Korean and contemporary dance, there is only a handful who majored in ballet, since the vast majority of those in ballet pursue dancing rather than choreography. In this context, James Jeon's work can be seen as vitally important in Korean ballet choreography.

The Seoul Ballet Theater that Jeon and Kim have led with such dedication since its founding in 1995 is in fact the only private professional ballet company in Korea. There are other private ballet companies, but they can hardly be called professional, due to an inability to assure their members of a steady income. In line with its quest to popularize ballet, the Seoul Ballet Theater has become well known for its unbounded enthusiasm for performance activities.

In the autumn of 2001, Jeon became the first in the Korean dance world to mount a production financed on a commercial basis: his ambitious ballet, "The Warehouse." Unfortunately, it failed to draw enough of an audience and closed earlier than planned. While Jeon was still feeling despair, a fortuitous opportunity presented itself. He secured a new base for his company at the Citizens' Hall of Gwacheon, an area close to Seoul with financially well-off and culturally sophisticated residents. Jeon welcomed this opportunity as a chance for a fresh start.

"It was in March 2002 that the Seoul Ballet Theater and I settled in Gwacheon," Jeon said. "After that, I started thinking about ways to make ballet more accessible to the general public. The first fruit of that effort was 'Ballet for Fun,' which we presented in July that year. By

1 James Jeon performing in "Self."
2 The rock ballet series "Being" is one of Jeon's most ambitious productions.

including explanations and demonstrations as part of our performance, we tried to plant in people's minds the idea that ballet is an accessible and enjoyable art form. This July, we plan to stage a new production based on the story of Snow White. 'The Nutcracker,' slated for the end of this year, is not merely a reproduction of a classic but a new adaptation, which we are thinking of including in our regular repertoire."

The bitter memory of the failure of "The Warehouse" might not have entirely disappeared from Jeon's face, but it has faded considerably. It seems that he will once again overcome his difficulties by virtue of his own character, cautious yet optimistic and above all, passionate.

Jeon is prolific. Fueled by his love for music, he has poured out a continuous stream of works, unbounded by subject matter and scope. In 1972 he immigrated to the United States, where he graduated from the dance department of the Juilliard School of Music. He performed with Maurice Bejart's ballet company before returning to Seoul in 1987 to join the Universal Ballet. His childhood years in America, his curiosity about things Korean, and his analytical view of his own experiences combined to produce an oeuvre of far-reaching diversity. His style, as well, ranges from neo-classical tendencies to a genre he calls "rock ballet."

Because of his prolific output and vivacious, uninhibited personality, it would be easy to misinterpret his works as based solely on his instincts and sensibilities. But James Jeon is more profound than these external appearances might suggest.

2

"Once I take on a new choreography project, I stop and think hard, not just about the dance and music, but about everything from lighting to scenery. And once I have figured everything out, I stick fast to my ideas," he said.

Widely regarded as his masterpiece, the rock ballet series "Being" reveals this strength of Jeon's character to the full. At first glance it appears to unfold easily with an upbeat mood, but in fact it went through a very difficult process of conceptualization and production.

Since it is not possible to examine all of Jeon's works here, a few examples have been chosen for discussion in this article, with a focus on their choreography and overall ambience.

Jeon's early work, "Three Moments" (1991) is in many ways reminiscent of George Balanchine's "Serenade."

From its underlying concept based on purely musical sensibilities aroused by Bach's "Concerto for Two Violins in E Major," to the basic color of its lighting, the work resembles "Serenade," which Balanchine created as an expression of his emotional reactions to Tchaikovsky's music.

Jeon explains: "'Three Moments' focuses on an articulation of movement with a sense of speed, along with a body approach or pose in which the dancers thrust their faces toward each other when the mood is subdued. It uses a staccato articulation in movement from low to high. To highlight separation in the articulation, I used more linear and angular positions, and above all, I paid great attention to the entrances and exits of the dancers so that there would always be something going on onstage."

Because of his prolific output and vivacious, uninhibited personality, it would be easy to misinterpret his works as based solely on his instincts and sensibilities. But James Jeon is more profound than these external appearances might suggest.

Perhaps that is why the piece conveys a sense of refined elegance as one movement begins before the previous one has ended. "City Light" (1993) features five young couples who are dressed in black and red costumes and holding crimson fans. It portrays their lives and loves, clinging and sensuous, and at times vivid and passionate.

"Being" arises from darker and deeper realms. An American-style outcry of a lonely rebel, it is not far removed from the world of James Dean. With its set decorated like a disco or rock café, rap music and dynamic dancing in break-dance mode, and frequent use of a freestyle movement that combines dancing and acting, "Being" stresses visual effect more than content. In this work, Jeon appears to be depicting in a modern setting the barriers separating him from himself as well as from others from an existential point of view. He achieves remarkable effects through the use of slides, motions like that of a boxer, sudden gunshots and two corpses, and the sound of extremely labored and tortured breathing.

However, Jeon does not overlook Korean elements. A remarkable product in this regard, "The Beggars" uses a distinctly Korean movement style, whether consciously or not. This reflects the diversity of Jeon's work in style, content and subject matter. Recently, his interests have turned overseas.

"In the summer of 2002, I was invited to choreograph 'Inner Moves' for the Nevada Ballet Theater in America. I used a bare stage and plain black and white costumes, expressing everything through music and movement only. The work was very well received. It might lead to more overseas projects," Jeon said.

Jeon does not allow himself a moment's rest. Endlessly experimenting, Jeon seems to believe his engagement with Gwacheon has been a most fortunate and mutually beneficial experience.

"Performance halls are springing up in many cities around Korea nowadays. But except in Seoul and some other big cities, these are just the hardware, with no software for operation. Most of them can't offer enough content to fill the stage and please the audience."

The Seoul Ballet Theater's residency in Gwacheon raises high hopes that provincial areas will have more cultural activities in the years ahead. The nation's dance circles may learn a valuable lesson from Pina Bausch who succeeded in turning the little German industrial city, Wuppertal, into a world-class center of dance, or the Centre Chorégraphique National that regularly invites talented choreographers to 20 cities across France.

Why should world-class artists not take up residence in Korean cities to transform them into artistic centers of international standing? In James Jeon, who overflows with passion as he steadily secures the practical means for realizing his ambitious dreams, I definitely see such a possibility.

Lee Jong-ho Dance Critic   **Park Sang-yun, Seo Heun-kang** Photographers

Korean Dancers on World Stages

Almost 100 foreign dance companies visited Korea to present over 300 performances during 2005, and this trend is likely to be repeated this year. What is especially noteworthy about these visiting foreign companies is that many of them have Korean members performing in leading roles.

One prominent example was the Stuttgart Ballet. The German ballet company attracted the greatest public interest among all foreign dance companies which visited Korea last year, primarily because its principal dancer was Korean ballerina Kang Sue-jin (Sue Jin Kang). In 1985, Kang became the first Asian to earn the top honors at the Prix de Lausanne, a prestigious international ballet competition, which led her to join the Stuttgart Ballet in 1986 as its youngest member. In 1999, she received the best female dancer award at Benois de la Danse, the dance world's version of the Academy Awards. An image of her ravaged toes shown in a TV documentary about her dance career is often cited as the kind of sacrifice required of an accomplished artist.

A look at the membership rosters of the world's leading ballet companies will reveal that a growing number of Koreans are performing actively on international stages. The American Ballet Theater, one of the most renowned U.S. ballet companies, has Seo Hee, also a winner of the Prix de Lausanne, who is following in the footsteps of Kang Ye-na (Yena Kang), the current principal dancer of Universal Ballet.

Korean dancers Ryu Ji-yeon (Ji Yeon Ryu) and Bae Joo-youn (Joo Youn Bae) have been performing for about 10 years with the Kirov Ballet and the Bolshoi Ballet, respectively, the two leading Russian ballet companies. Both of these dancers went to Russia to study at the Vaganova Ballet Academy, a leading international ballet school in St. Petersburg, and earned fame by being invited to join these

Kim Joo-won, a principal dancer of the Korean National Ballet Company, received the Benois de la Danse award in 2006 for her role in "Don Quixote."

prestigious companies right after their graduation.

Korean ballet dancers are active in Northern and Western Europe as well. Jun Eun-sun, a former principal dancer of the Universal Ballet, is now with the Royal Swedish Ballet. Kim Seh-yun (Seh Yun Kim), another former principal dancer of the Universal Ballet, is presently a member of the largest ballet company in Switzerland, the Zurich Ballet, which promoted her to principal dancer last year. Kim Ji-young (Ji Young Kim) and Kim Yong-geol (Yong Geol Kim), who regularly performed as principal dancers of the Korean National Ballet Company in the mid-1990s, have also joined major ballet companies in Europe. Kim Ji-young is a soloist of the Dutch National Ballet, while Kim Yong-geol is a member of the Paris Opera Ballet. Jang Yoo-jin, who joined the Essen Ballet of Germany in 2003, has risen rapidly through the corps de ballet and will be playing the lead role of Odette in "Swan Lake" this season. In addition, Lee So-ra (Sora Lee) is a member of the Lyon Opera Ballet of France, and Han Sang-yi (Sang-yi Han) performs with the Monte Carlo Ballet in Monaco.

Among Korea's male dancers who have made their way onto the global stage, Kim Yong-geol has especially distinguished himself. He began by passing the apprentice-member audition of the Paris Opera Ballet, which is the world's oldest classical ballet company, and for six months, he attended classes and jumped at every opportunity to perform on stage. Then, in an audition where 50 talented dancers from around the world competed, he was selected as a member of the company and has since been promoted to a soloist. His step-by-step career advancement reflects how fertile the Korean dance environment has become to nurture internationally competitive performers. Other Korean dancers who are active overseas include Seo Dong-hyun (Dong Hyun Seo), with the National Ballet of Canada, and Kwak Kyu-dong (Kyu

Dong Kwak), with the Nevada Ballet Theatre.

Recently, more Korean dancers are also appearing regularly with modern dance companies worldwide. For example, Kim Na-young (Nayoung Kim) has already been performing with the Pina Baush Tanztheater Wuppertal for 10 years. Jeon Yeon-hee dances with the Saarbrücken Ballet in Germany, while Kim Nam-jin is a member of Les Ballet C. de la B, the most prominent modern dance company in Belgium. Meanwhile, Yeo Hyo-sung performs for the Ultima Vez, and Jeon Young-ja for the Nederlands Dans Theater.

Some of these performers, after a lengthy and successful dance career, have gone on to serve in related professions, such as trainers or choreographers. Hur Yong-soon, who studied at the Princess Grace Academy of Classical

Dance ahead of Kang Sue-jin, is a case in point. Following her notable appearances as a principal dancer of the Zurich Ballet and the Düsseldorf Ballet, she has become a professional trainer and choreographer.

Ever since Kang Sue-jin proved the ability of Korean dancers by joining the Stuttgart Ballet in 1986, an increasing number of young Korean dancers have sought to advance to the international stage. But by the mid-1990s, only a handful had attained notable success. Recently, performing with a foreign company has become more commonplace for Koreans. The number of Korean dancers working with overseas companies has surged noticeably in the 2000s. Currently, about 120 Korean dancers are performing in foreign countries, of which about a half are professional dancers belonging to leading international

The number of Korean dancers working with overseas companies has surged noticeably in the 2000s. Currently, about 120 Korean dancers are performing in foreign countries, of which about a half are professional dancers belonging to leading international companies.

1 Kim Yong-geol, a member of the Paris Opera Ballet, performs in "Giselle."
   © IPOP
2 Kim Na-young, a member of the Pina Baush Tanztheater Wuppertal, performs
   in "Solo for Two."

companies. There are several principal dancers with top-tier ballet companies.

There are several factors behind this growing success of Korean dancers abroad. First, there are now more opportunities to participate in international competitions. Second, an increasing number of Korean dancers have been receiving top awards at prestigious international contests. Third, the Internet's proliferation has served to disseminate abundant information on dance, thus providing dancers with more chances to audition for foreign companies. Fourth, the ongoing exchanges with foreign dance companies, through international dance festivals held in Korea and performances of visiting foreign dance companies here, have assured Korean dancers that they may audition overseas. And above all, there is now worldwide recognition of the excellent technique and artistic flair of Korean dancers.

Young Korean dancers frequently capture top honors at international competitions these days. In July, five Koreans won awards at the Varna International Ballet Competition in Bulgaria, where dancers from 32 countries competed. They include Choi Young-gyu and Hong Hyang-gi, who won silver and bronze medals, respectively, in the junior dance category; Lee Young-do and Park Seul-gi, who won bronze medals in the senior dance category; and Min Sue-kyung, who received first prize in the creativity category for modern dance. This impressive showing in Varna was built on the momentum from the 2005 Prix de Lausanne competition, in which Koreans captured four awards. Park Sae-eun, who won the 2006 USA International Ballet Competition, is another promising Korean dancer who will soon debut on the world stage.

This standard of excellence was further bolstered in 2006, when Kim Joo-won, the principal dancer and 10-year member of the Korean National Ballet Company, shared the coveted Prix Benois de la Danse with a Russian. As Korean dancers continue to earn high marks at international events, their appearances on the global stage will subsequently increase as well. Their presence will not only elevate the stature of Korean dance professionals but also the image of Korean culture and arts in the international community.

Jang Gwang-ryul Arts Critic   **Lee Eun-joo** Photographer

Nonverbal Performance Groups Garner Global Acclaim

"Nanta," the pioneering nonverbal production in Korea, has animated storylines presented with dynamic beats rooted in native Korean percussion music. It marked one million foreign viewers in September 2006.

Nonverbal performance in Korea has a short history of only some 10 years, beginning with the launch of "Nanta" (also known as "Cookin'"). Korean performance art, though a late entry to the ranks of leading international nonconventional theater groups, such as STOMP, Blue Man Group and Cirque du Soleil, has since attracted considerable attention from audiences at home and abroad. In September 2006, "Nanta" broke the one-million mark in terms of the number of foreign viewers, while "Jump" celebrated the opening of its own theater, which will be dedicated to the group's performances on a long-term basis. An evaluation of the factors behind the phenomenal success of these two forerunners of Korea's innovative stage arts reveals a number of common characteristics.

The first that the two groups discovered was the global appeal and competitiveness of Korea's traditional culture. While "Nanta" focused on *samulnori* (traditional-style percussion music performed with drums and gongs), "Jump" developed martial arts-related themes. This popularization of aspects of Korea's traditional culture through the nonverbal genre helped differentiate Korean nonverbal performances on the world stage. Moreover, neither "Nanta" nor "Jump" was satisfied with simply displaying the artistic elements of Korea's traditional percussion music and martial arts. They further sought to express the joys and sorrows of everyday life, which might occur in the kitchen or ordinary family situations, through animated drama. They created a model for success based on an ability to integrate traditional Korean cultural themes into their nonverbal performances, which are presented through comedic storytelling.

The two groups have also set foreign audience milestones for the nation's performing arts industry. Although these groups debuted in Korea, they both envisioned making their way onto the global stage on the strength of their successful appearances at the well-known Edinburgh Fringe Festival. Indeed, they went on to gain widespread acclaim during world tours, and then used this momentum to establish exclusive theaters at home for staging their shows on a continuing basis.

Thanks to the active marketing of their shows as part of package tours for visitors to Korea, the two groups have enjoyed growing popularity both at home and abroad.

Buoyed by the notable success of "Nanta," a number of new performance groups have sought to follow in their footsteps, but the results have been mixed. Tokebi Storm and DoodRock offer entertaining performances; however, they have failed to clearly distinguish themselves from the "Nanta" brand of nonverbal theater. On the other hand, "Jump" highlighted elements of martial arts, rather than percussion instruments, which enabled it to create a unique image. After this decade-long process, Korea's nonverbal performance scene is now building a platform for another takeoff, seeking to capitalize on the recent emergence of the sensational B-Boy culture.

Although the B-Boy culture has largely been considered a youth-oriented subculture in the country, Korean B-Boys have recently dominated several international competitions, earning a reputation as being the world's foremost break dancers. Entertainment agencies have come to realize this and are thus racing to launch a host of new performances for local audiences. "The Ballerina Who Loved a B-Boy," which has enjoyed steadily growing popularity over the past year since its opening at a theater near Hongik University, a mecca for youth culture, is now encountering intensified competition from "B-Boy Korea," created by the agency that represents "Nanta," as well as Picnic, the management agency of "Jump."

"Jump" has contributed greatly to the B-Boy syndrome. Whereas "Nanta" is centered on the Korean sounds of folk percussion music, "Jump" performers execute the high-precision techniques of martial arts routines. The recent clamor about B-Boy culture is due to their truly extraordinary movements, which are perhaps even more physically demanding than those of martial arts. Although Korea's B-Boy culture is not rooted in the local tradition, the stellar reputation of Korean B-Boys has been firmly established worldwide, making this genre another form of theater art.

However, the performing arts watchers are cautious about the long-term prospects of B-Boy dramas, because

Korean B-Boy culture attracts keen attention from the nonverbal performing arts industry. The spellbinding break dance techniques are integrated into the existing performing arts such as ballet, mime and traditional dance.

although there seem to be tremendous possibilities for successful ventures, competition has been extremely fierce from the outset and the market can only support the most popular productions. Ultimately, it is likely that a small number of performances might survive, while the others are doomed to failure. Perhaps aware of this harsh reality, the agencies that promote B-Boy performances are being especially careful and varied in their marketing strategies.

The agency behind "Nanta," which is leading the way in exploring the overseas markets for Korean innovative theater, seeks to apply the lessons learned from its trial-and-error experiences in developing the international competitiveness of "B-Boy Korea." For now, its strategy calls for refinement of the show through long-term per-

formances in Korea before embarking on overseas tours so that a highly competitive product can be developed for foreign audiences. The agency representing "Jump," on the other hand, which had a later start than "Nanta" in entering overseas markets, is taking a more aggressive approach by staging its premiere overseas. They are striving to produce a work that will first be successful abroad and then make a triumphant return to Korea.

There are also concerns about the uniqueness and competitiveness of B-Boy-related performances. Already, there are several shows that combine B-Boy dancing with traditional instruments or comic drama, but most industry experts are assuming a wait-and-see attitude about whether these efforts can rekindle the popular interest in

Not only B-Boy culture but other forms of innovative theater as well should attain a more mature level by developing good subject matters with universal appeal and constantly engaging in creative experimentation. Korea's nonverbal performance art finds itself standing at a crossroads, while preparing for another decade of thriving performances on world stages.

"Jump" was the No. 1 box-office attraction at the 2005 Edinburgh Fringe Festival. It combines Eastern martial arts with comedic elements to create an exciting form of entertainment.

the fresh and charming appeal of the original B-Boy culture. There are also those who worry that if these fads fail to exhibit a new form of artistry, this could well result in a loss of the opportunity to transform the exceptional talent of Korean B-Boys into high value-added performances on the world stage.

The praiseworthy achievements of "Nanta" and "Jump" have greatly contributed to the fast development and growth of nonverbal performance art in Korea. In contrast, the recent efforts to combine B-Boy culture with other forms of entertainment are now at only a fledgling phase. But the accumulated production and marketing know-how will enable new productions to be introduced to the market in a shorter time frame. Not only B-Boy culture but other forms of innovative theater as well should attain a more mature level by developing good subject matters with universal appeal and constantly engaging in creative experimentation.

Korea's nonverbal performance art finds itself standing at a crossroads, while preparing for another decade of thriving performances on world stages. It is hoped that the recent contribution of B-Boy culture will result in richer styles of performing arts, thereby creating new momentum for innovative theater of higher standards.

Kim Jong-whee Culture Critic   **Ahn Hong-beom** Photographer

Kim Min-gi

Activist Songwriter Turns Musical Director

Kim Min-gi, the proprietor of Hakchon Theater, is a celebrity known to Koreans of all generations. His notable career has included many vicissitudes and achievements. Singer-songwriter of the biggest hits of the 1970s, such as "Morning Dew," "The Little Pond" and "Friends," which are still popular today, he is also remembered as an activist who stood up to the country's military regimes. The late 1970s and early 1980s found him working at farms and factories, and then presenting his musical "The Factory Lights." Since the 1990s, he has been active as a musical director and theater manager.

The changes wrought by Kim on the country's performing arts scene are exceptionally worthy of praise. Though regarded as an archetypal activist, he remains untainted by political power and thus his fame shines even more brightly.

Though reluctant to talk about himself, Kim agreed to sit down with me for an interview. We talked mainly about the experiences that have made him what he is today and the musical "Line 1," which will mark its 2,000th performance this autumn.

CHOE JUN-HO: I'm curious to know what you were like as a child.

KIM MIN-GI: The first thing I can remember is when I was about three. When the grown-ups asked me how old I was between the Solar New Year and Lunar New Year, I got all confused. When I was four or five, my greatest fear was death. Death was already all around me, and when I tried to understand it rationally, I grew afraid. What happens after death? I kept wondering, and I got worried. That was when I started staring at the ground and drawing pictures.

Around then, I had an inspiration from a sign shop in our neighborhood. In their spare time, the people who worked at the shop painted a wall black and then decorated it with stars and human figures in white. I got an inspiration from it. In other words, my path in life was decided. As the youngest of 10 children, I got much attention from the family, and I ended up entering the College of Fine Arts at Seoul National University to learn about what I wanted to do: painting pictures.

CHOE: At college, I understand, you devoted yourself

passionately to painting, and after your graduation exhibition you were expected to become a leading artist of your generation. How did you happen to change course and pursue a musical career instead?

KIM: Before my college days, I had learned classical guitar. Once I entered college, I worked hard at my painting and played guitar just for fun. I loved music, and one day, a contemporary of mine from high school, Im Mun-il, who was a DJ for the Christian Broadcasting System, asked me to play guitar and accompany his girlfriend Yang Hee-un, who was a singer. So I embarked on my music career just by chance. As I became familiar with the form of pop songs, I grew more confident and started to write my own songs, which I either gave to Yang Hee-un or sang myself. But the military regime banned the broadcast and sale of my songs, and my composing activities dwindled.

CHOE: Living as a fugitive for so long, you couldn't live a normal life in society. What are your recollections of that period?

KIM: Living in hiding or on the run would have meant

"In this age with a dire need for creative imagination, when everything is profit-motivated, I'd like to express the world's values as seen by an older person, through a show for children, like those that used to provide us with consolation in difficult times."

1 The rock musical "Line 1," adopted from the German original and directed by Kim Min-gi, opened at Hakcheon Theater in May 1994 and marked its 2,000th performance on November 9, 2003.
2 Kim says he hopes to devote himself to drama for children and youth in the future.

too much trouble for my friends and family, so I never once went into hiding. I went as far away as possible, but I registered my new address. I felt far away from the people I knew and the world of songs. Since I couldn't get a regular job, from the mid- to late 1970s I spent five years in the countryside doing farm work. After that I got a job at a factory under an assumed name, because I couldn't use my own... I think I did all this just to make a living. "The Factory Lights" was made based on my experiences during those days.

CHOE: You always speak so modestly, but in fact your activities were very significant in terms of bringing public attention to factory conditions and the related labor movement. So, what was the reason for your moving into theater after that?

KIM: In the late 1980s, I was director of the Yeonwoo Theater Company. Having become involved with drama and performance, I was able to serve as a bridge when the Yeonwoo Theater Company was in the process of taking over what is now Hakchon Theater. For some reason or other, the company wasn't able to take over the theater, and being in the middle, I solved the problem by taking over the theater myself. That was in 1991 — but it also involved an unexpected turn of events. To take over the theater, I suddenly needed money, so I signed a recording contract with Seoul Record Company that brought me 50 million won, enabling me to take over the theater. In 1993, a 3-CD set was released, and to my surprise, it earned me 200 million won in royalties, enough to pay off two-thirds of my debt.

CHOE: I bought quite a few copies of that album myself to give to others.

KIM: Oh, I'm sorry! (Laughter)

CHOE: While operating the theater, you planned some-

1 Kim and the former East German dissident singer-songwriter Wolf Biermann in 2005.
2 A three-CD set of Kim's songs, released in 1993.

thing quite unusual, didn't you?

KIM: Knowing nothing but music, the first thing I did was to organize the "Song Seekers" live concerts. In 1991, Seo Tai-ji was making huge hits, and the music industry was all about media and recording studios. By promoting live concerts in small theaters, I helped the audiences realize, albeit belatedly, that the sound from the latest speakers could never match the live sound from the six strings of an acoustic guitar. With "Song Seekers" I was able to make ends meet, and the industry soon found its way to Daehang-no Street, where live concert venues began to spring up.

In the 1980s, everything had been about either mass gatherings or the media, and I revived what both of these had neglected: the intimate meeting of music and audience. Then, musicians like Kim Gwang-seok further promoted live concerts at small theaters, and the theater district was swamped with "song strummers." Besides, it didn't make sense to keep renting theaters, and it suddenly

occurred to me that if I took the lead myself I could save some labor costs. And so I produced the musical "Line 1."

CHOE: It may have started by chance, but the small-theater musical was notable for its many contributions. Why did you decide to use live music right from the first performance in 1993?

KIM: It wasn't due to any particular reason. It was simply out of musical consideration. I didn't like singing to recorded accompaniment, not to mention lip-synching, so although it would cost more, I chose to give the musical the live feeling that comes from even a single guitar or a few instruments. Ultimately, I was producing a work keeping my own style, and if anything about it was different from the past, it was that I had to consider the practical problem of how to feed my extended theatrical family. In a way, I wasn't so much managing a business as giving the audience a show that they would enjoy. "Line 1" has grossed some 5 billion won (about $4 million), enabling

us to hire a large number of cast members and all of us to stay alive and produce new works.

CHOE: I believe Hakchon Theater has contributed greatly to the musical scene, especially in regard to the training of actors and staff members.

KIM: You could see it that way. A number of actors have passed through Hakchon. For the last 10 years, I have insisted that proper royalties be paid and performers be selected through open auditions. These practices have since been spreading throughout the performing arts world. My concept hasn't changed. First, the schools plant the seeds of future artists, then I bring them here and provide a seedbed for their talent to blossom. That's the concept behind my theater and my productions. In director Lim Kwon-taik's latest film which will open this autumn, 80 percent of the cast have acted here.

CHOE: What are your current concerns and plans for the future?

KIM: While pondering creation and the universe, I've been touched by Hindu philosophy. I also find the universal antiquity in folk legends and fairy tales very interesting. In this age with a dire need for creative imagination, when everything is profit-motivated, I'd like to express the world's values as seen by an older person, through a show for children, like those that used to provide us with consolation in difficult times. I have seen how Germany is building marvelous theaters for children and youth. This children's musical was originally scheduled to open in the autumn, but I have put it off until early next year. Now that so many people are rushing to create children's shows to make money, I hope I won't be misunderstood as doing the same thing.

CHOE: Thank you for sharing your valuable time.

Choe Jun-ho Drama Critic / Professor of Drama, Korea National University of Arts

Musicians

Kim Duk-soo
Dynamic Percussionist and Korea's Cultural Envoy

In a fairy tale from my childhood, I remember there was a *dokkaebi* (a kind of goblin) who could make at will any precious items like gold and silver appear out of thin air by simply tapping his mallet. Although not in the realm of fantasy, Kim Duk-soo, a master of traditional Korean percussion music, says that he often feels he is like a dokkaebi. Suddenly appearing here and there, like a bolt of lightning, Kim has passionately performed with his drum for audiences across the world, receiving invariably enthusiastic applause at every venue.

Just like a dokkaebi who simply taps his mallet, Kim Duk-soo, the maestro, has thrilled his audiences everywhere. His zealous dedication to *samulnori* (percussion quartet) enables him to establish an instant bond with anyone in earshot of the exhilarating sounds of his ingenious group, SamulNori. His vibrant performances have helped to heighten awareness of Korea and its culture among numerous countries and peoples around the world. Indeed, it is impossible for anyone not to be aroused by the rhythmic clanging, clashing and thumping sounds of the four powerful samul nori instruments: the *buk* (barrel drum), *janggo* (double-headed hourglass drum), *kkwaenggwari* (small gong) and *jing* (large gong).

In fact, the global media has dubbed Kim as "Mr. Janggo," whose frenetic style of drum playing is helping to spread the dynamic spirit of Korea throughout the world.

Kim notes: "I play my janggo with the same kind of mindset that drives a 100-meter sprinter to strive to improve his personal best time, if only by one thousandth of a second." With some 4,000 performances in 60 countries highlighting his personal record, he can also be regarded as Korea's foremost cultural ambassador.

Kim, who stands at the forefront of the world of samulnori, a rather recently coined moniker for the harmonized sounds of thunder, rain, clouds and wind produced by the four percussion instruments, fully deserves his reputation as a world-class traditional artist. Encouraged by his father to play the janggo from a young age, Kim was recognized as a child prodigy from early on. In 1978, he created a new genre of percussion music that has since come to be known as "*samulnori*" which, though rooted in the traditional farmers' band music (*pungmul*) mostly played outdoors, was rearranged to be performed on a formal stage. This turned out to be a turning point in the history of Korean music, for which Kim was selected by the Chosun Ilbo, a leading national daily, as one of the 50

most influential Koreans since the nation's liberation from Japanese colonial rule in 1945.

Few other developments in the music world have been quite as revolutionary as the emergence of SamulNori in 1978. The young musicians' group resurrected the native sense of musical rhythm that for long had been dormant within the Korean people. It also helped to introduce a form of traditional Korean music to the international community and paved the way for two-way exchanges between Korean musicians and their foreign counterparts.

After having taken the domestic performing arts scene by storm, Kim Duk-soo and his SamulNori troupe began to perform in such disparate venues as the United Nations, ASEM Summit, the Wailing Wall of Jerusalem, Central Park in New York City, a munitions warehouse in Munich, Tokyo's Shibuya district, and most recently, Arbil (Irbil), Iraq, where Korea's Zaytun division is stationed. All of these performances are undertaken in accordance with time-honored Korean customs.

Kim says: "Our performance for the Zaytun division in February was nothing out of the ordinary. We always conduct certain rituals before every performance. These include preparing a ritual table and lighting candles. The supreme commander of the allied troops, and the commanders of the U.S., Japanese and Australian troops each bowed respectfully, while the wife of the commander of the Zaytun division came up on stage to participate in our ritual. It was not until we concluded this Korean-style ceremony that we started our performance."

The group's overseas activities are not limited to stage performances. They also include lectures on samulnori, which have led to the formation of local samulnori groups around the world. "Samulnorian" clubs, of fans with a keen interest in the native Korean music style, have been formed wherever the group has performed. This year, the group conducted a workshop in Berlin for ethnic Koreans residing in Germany, from April 10–17. They will soon be returning to Germany to participate in the 2006 FIFA World Cup festivities.

"The manner in which we introduce our traditions to the world is very important," Kim said. "We therefore plan to establish a Korean cultural village in Germany that will be responsible for hosting performances and festivals so that Korean culture can be regularly promoted.

1 The four instruments forming a typical *samul nori* ensemble. They are, from left, *kkwaenggari* (small gong) representing the sound of thunder; *jing* (large gong) making the sound of wind; *buk* (barrel drum) for the sound of clouds; and *janggo* (double-headed hourglass drum) the sound of rain.
2 Kim Duk-soo has devoted himself to the introduction of traditional Korean music to the world and paved the way for two-way exchanges between Korean and foreign musicians.

1

2

After having taken the domestic performing arts scene by storm, Kim Duk-soo and his SamulNori troupe began to perform in such disparate venues as the United Nations, ASEM Summit, the Wailing Wall of Jerusalem, Central Park in New York City, a munitions warehouse in Munich, Tokyo's Shibuya district, and most recently, Arbil (Irbil), Iraq, where Korea's Zaytun division is stationed.

Of course, we will perform to help cheer on our national team at the World Cup matches in major German cities. I think this will be an outstanding example of Korean-style cheering culture."

The Asia Society, a leading U.S. institution dedicated to introducing Asian culture among the American public, has invited Kim's SamulNori troupe to perform for U.S. audiences on five separate occasions, thus making an exception to its stated policy of not inviting the same group more than once. Beate Gordon, the society's director of the performing arts, once described SamulNori's performance as "a major event." At the heart of any music is its rhythm; however, the dynamism of SamulNori is so frenzied that it does not lend itself to measurement by a metronome.

When asked about his most memorable concert abroad, Kim cites a performance at the Percussive Arts Society International Convention (PASIC-82) held on November 19, 1982. Morris Lang, one of the steering committee members of PASIC, had the following to say about the SamulNori troupe: "After having listened to that incredible performance carried out by only four individuals, I realized that I needed to learn more about Korean culture. I could see why audiences the world over are so captivated by their sound after only a few minutes have passed."

Samulnori has thus become a most popular form of traditional Korean music at home and abroad. Nowadays, samulnori troupes are regularly invited to appear on TV, while their CDs enjoy widespread popularity. It is truly remarkable that this music style has become such a vital aspect of everyday life in Korea in a brief period of less than 30 years. Indeed, the majority of Korean elementary schools now maintain a folk percussion group or club. There are about 300 samulnori troupes that perform on a professional basis, as well as another 2,000 or so amateur groups.

Since its inception, Kim's SamulNori troupe has active-

1 SamulNori gives a joint performance with the Ansan Municipal Korean Orchestra at the Ansan Culture and Arts Center.
2 Kim Duk-soo and SamulNori have performed and given lectures on their unique music genre, leading to the formation of local amateur groups in many countries.

ly pursued collaboration with artists from other genres. These collaborative efforts with artists of jazz, rock, pop, modern dance, Western classical music and traditional Korean music have helped to establish a globalized form of samulnori. The troupe has shared stages with numerous Korean and foreign performers at home and abroad, and produced CDs that have been sold in overseas markets.

As a musician, Kim maintains an open-mindedness that enables him to appreciate what different styles of music can offer to enrich his own musical sensibilities. These interactions, with diverse kinds of music and musicians from East and West, have helped Kim acquire a highly prolific style. One of the most meaningful experiences for Kim and his colleagues was getting to know Red Sun, a multinational jazz group comprised of Wolfgang Puschnig (saxophone, clarinet, flute), Rick Iannacone (electric guitar), Jamaaladeen Tacuma (bass guitar) and Linda Sharrock (vocals). The collaboration between SamulNori and Red Sun not only led to the development of

a new genre of music, but has also resulted in joint international performances and the production of three CDs entitled "Red Sun/SamulNori."

"In the future, I would like to offer a comprehensive performing art that features not only percussion quartet but also integrates traditional performing arts genres, such as masked dance and marionette plays. I want to lead one of the most cutting-edge musical groups of this era to showcase the cultural energy of our nation that is overflowing with vibrancy," Kim said.

Kim is also working on a new cultural program to bring Korea's traditional art forms to the stage. Next year will mark the 50th anniversary of his debut. To mark the occasion, Kim plans to publish a book about his 50-year career and present many performances, including a major tour of Europe, the United States and South America, where he has already performed extensively.

Hyun Kyung-chae Music Critic/Member, Arts Council Korea

Ahn Suk-sun

Leading *Pansori* Singer of the Modern Era

A hn Suk-seon is indisputably the preeminent *pansori* virtuoso of our time. This is not because of her widespread popularity. Nor is it because she is a darling of the local media. By no means is it because of her immeasurable success and the numerous awards and citations that she has received at home and abroad. As everyone knows, it is not enough to merely sing beautifully to be recognized as a master musician; one needs the ability to project one's innermost spiritual realm through music to move audiences. Only then can one be acknowledged as a masterful vocalist worthy of critical acclaim.

The "innermost spiritual realm" can be referred to as *esprit d'art*, a total immersion in one's endeavor, or simply, intensity. It could also be thought of as perseverance that outlasts all others. It can be called effort, or the mindset of a professional. Most singers, however, cannot overcome this barrier to the spiritual realm, because it is impossible to do so without enormous sacrifice and self-motivation.

For this reason, try as they may, the vast majority of singers will advance no further than the level of technical mastery. Within Korea's traditional culture scene, there seems to be a number of well-known pansori singers, but it is difficult to find truly great musicians. And among

these rare virtuoso singers, the best performer is without a doubt Ahn Suk-seon, who combines incomparable vocal talent with boundless spiritual strength.

On a pleasant day, as gentle breezes played a prelude to spring, I visited Ahn at her office at the National Theater of Korea, where she serves as director of the National Changgeuk Company. Unlike her usual taciturn demeanor, Ahn was quite expressive as she spoke frankly about the path she has trod along.

"I remember the days of my youth, in my hometown of Namwon, she recalled. "I used to think of the pond at Gwanghallu Garden as the Indangsu Sea, into which the devoted daughter Sim Cheong threw herself. If someone had offered me some rice, I think I could have sacrificed myself just as the poor girl did. That's how poor we were."

In truth, during those hard times when Korea was a poor agricultural society, poverty was prevalent and almost everyone led a hand-to-mouth existence. The most difficult period of the year was the "barley hump" around April and May, after the rice supply was depleted and before the barley harvest began, when families were forced to get by on grass roots and tree bark. It isn't surprising

that Ahn's family experienced similar hardship. Her father died early, her grandmother was bedridden with paralysis, and her mother was left to raise five children and manage the household on her own. Even her older brother had to sell candies on the street, and there was little time for her to enjoy herself.

Fortunately, Ahn inherited her musical talent — one of her relatives was a well-known *gayageum* (12-string zither) player, another was a pansori singer, and there were others who were involved with Korean folk music. She naturally pursued a path of Korean music and joined the Chunhyang Women's Art Troupe, traveling around the country and learning about the tough entertainment world from a young age.

"I was yet to reach the age when I could truly appreciate music. I was dragged along against my will to perform at one place after another, and it was not a very enjoyable experience. It seemed to be an exhausting way of life. But when I look back, I should probably have to admit that it was an experience and opportunity that no amount of money could buy," she said.

Ahn was absolutely right; it would be no exaggeration to say that the key to her success was deeply rooted in those experiences. And this is also the source of a glaring deficiency of most pansori singers as well as other traditional musicians who are nurtured under today's so-called systematized educational programs, including those at universities. Although they may possess outstanding musi-

1 Virtuoso *pansori* singer Ahn Suk-sun performs on stage.
2 An acclaimed singer, Ahn splits her time directing the National Changgeuk (Folk Opera) Company, affiliated with the National Theater of Korea.

cal talent and ability, most musicians of the new generation seem to be somewhat lacking in their on-stage skills. For the most part, this is because they have not personally experienced the world from which the folk music genres originated. Accordingly, they can offer an accurate rendition of the notes on their sheet music, but cannot read between the lines and convey the true sentiments of an age long gone.

Therein lies the reason Ahn can truly stand out. Though she will sing the same lyrics, in her music dwells a tenacious power from her real-life struggle that is capable of transcending mere sound. This inner realm reflects the joys and sorrows of the wandering entertainers and the pungency of the unpretentious and tough life of the common people. Simply, the singing of the new-generation musicians is like the flowers that have been cultivated in a greenhouse, while Ahn's singing is like the hardy wildflowers that must weather all hardships to survive.

As I relished the fragrance of a cup of green tea, the sorrowful strains of Sarasate's "*Zigeunerweisen*" (Gypsy Airs) suddenly flowed through my mind. Just as the wandering bands of gypsies have left their mark on many aspects of European culture, the Korean itinerant per-

forming groups have played an instrumental role in shaping our folk culture as well. This was true of the *sadang pae* performing groups, who earned their livelihood by entertaining the common people, as well as the *changgeuk* (folk opera) troupes of the early 20th century, who played a definitive role in keeping alive the pulse of traditional music genres, such as pansori, the narrative epic chants. Ahn spent her formative years dreaming of becoming a famous singer while traveling with these roaming entertainers.

Then, I asked Ahn what her childhood nickname was.

"The grownups would call me 'Sassy' or 'Little Caterpillar.' They called me 'Sassy' because I was kind of impertinent and always joking around."

Ahn projects an image of a person of considerable intelligence with a sense of detachment. But contrary to this impression, on the inside she is surprisingly personable and sentimental. Sassy contrasts with her other nickname, Little Caterpillar. A caterpillar clings to the underside of leaves and will startle people. It suggests Ahn's intelligence and upright character.

The two nicknames are not unrelated to her music career. If she did not have an impertinent, yet sensitive

Though she will sing the same lyrics, in her music dwells a tenacious power from her real-life struggle that is capable of transcending mere sound. This inner realm reflects the joys and sorrows of the wandering entertainers and the pungency of the unpretentious and tough life of the common people.

nature, she would not have been able to touch the heartstrings of her audiences with her unique strength that comes from the ups and downs of her life experiences. And, if she did not have the tenacious survival instinct of the caterpillar, she would have been swept under by the waves of adversity long before becoming a towering figure that she is today.

Ahn went on, "Having spent my whole youth on the stage, I wandered much spiritually. I was able to overcome this period of wandering and doubt thanks to my two beloved teachers: Bak Gwi-hui (1921–1993) and Kim So-hui (1917–1995)."

Many Koreans might recall the two musicians were both the popular matriarchs who led the world of traditional folk music during the latter half of the 20th century. Bak was a highly acclaimed *gayageum* player and singer, while Kim dominated the pansori world. Ahn noted: "I learned musical skills from them, but more than the skills I learned about the human virtues and professional mindset that an artist must have."

While her music has attained a sublime standard of refinement, Ahn has never lost the admiration and respect of her audience. She said she has consistently devoted herself to the all-consuming task of committing her life to her music single-heartedly.

These are by no means empty words. People who know about her life and have enjoyed her performances would heartily agree. She has not been spoiled by the enormous admiration showered upon her over the years, nor does she tailor her singing to perceptions of what today's audiences might prefer. Like her childhood nickname, Little Caterpillar, she coldly rejects anything outside her music, while being fully immersed in her musical pursuits and tenaciously advancing toward the goals she has set for her career.

Pansori is a Korean musical form presented by a single performer, who sings and acts, narrating the story (*aniri*) to the accompaniment of a single drummer. The stories are taken from classic tales. It resembles Western operas, except that a single performer takes on all the singing, acting and narrating roles. A single performance can run from four hours, for shorter pieces, to over eight hours for longer works, as in the case of "The Song of Chunhyang" (*Chunhyang ga*). However, even for an eight-hour performance, there is no intermission or break for the solo singer, who performs continuously from the beginning to the end. It is this very perseverance and endurance, this archetypal characteristic that lies beneath all of Korea's traditional culture, which is at the core of Ahn's singing. A cluster of wildflowers on the canvas of her uncompromising professional mindset that sassily depicts the simple sentiments of the Korean people — this is the essence of Ahn Suk-seon's virtuosity.

Hanh Myung-hee Director, Imisi Academy for Korean Music Culture
Ahn Hong-beom Photographer

Chung Myung-whun
Maestro Envisions the World United by Music

The success of young Korean musicians on the world stage of classical music is truly noteworthy. Korean *wunderkinder*, such as Sarah Chang, Han-na Chang and Daniel Lee, for example, are more strongly motivated and established than their counterparts from other neighboring countries. Therefore, major recording multinationals such as EMI and Deutsche Grammophon make annual scouting trips to Korea to look for the latest talents.

As is widely known, conductor Chung Myung-whun was one of the first generation of Korean musicians to succeed overseas. He and his sisters, violinist Chung Kyung-wha and cellist Chung Myung-wha, were the first Koreans to make their names known in the world classical music scene. They were also the pioneers who blazed the way for the new generation of Korean musicians to successfully debut on the world stage.

Known as the "Chung Trio," their achievements abroad have brought honor to the Chung family and to their motherland, Korea. Their parents, who immigrated to the United States and ran a cold noodles restaurant in order to support their children's education, raised three world-class musicians in one generation. Their mother later told this remarkable story in an autobiography, which became a bestseller in Korea.

Unlike Kyung-wha, who lives in New York, and Myung-wha, who has settled in Korea as a professor at Korean National University of Arts, Myung-whun has been active as a conductor in Europe. Born in 1953, he began playing the piano at age five and by age seven, he had already performed with the Seoul Philharmonic Orchestra. After immigrating to the United States with his family, Chung attended the Juilliard School of Music where he majored in piano and earned awards at leading international competitions such as the Chopin Piano

Chung Myung-whun carries on his successful career overseas as conductor for some of the world's finest orchestras.

"Each time, in each country, I could clearly sense the 'local flavor,' the tastes of the people. The very moment I lift the baton, however, all regional characteristics become meaningless. It is the same with the Tokyo Philharmonic. In that moment there are no Japanese, no Koreans. There is only music."

Competition in Warsaw, the ARD International Music Competition in Munich and the Tchaikovsky Competition in Moscow. Chung thus seemed to be treading a path to success like his elder sister Kyung-wha, who was quickly establishing herself as a world-famous violinist.

While performing primarily as a pianist until the 1980s, Chung also served as an assistant conductor for the Los Angeles Philharmonic Orchestra in 1978, which led to his appointment as music director and principal conductor for Germany's Saarbrücken Radio Symphony Orchestra, thus launching his career as a conductor. Then, after having worked with such prestigious orchestras as the Berlin Philharmonic, Los Angeles Philharmonic, Munich Philharmonic and London Philharmonic, Chung was named to succeed Daniel Barenboim as music director and permanent conductor of the world-renowned Bastille Opera Orchestra. At the Bastille podium in Paris, a world center of arts and culture, Chung was now front and center of the global classical music community. In recognition of his musical prowess, Chung received numerous awards, including the "Man of the Year" award given by the French Theater and Music Critics Association in 1991, the French national medal "Légion d'Honneur" in 1992, and the Classical Music Victory Award in 1995. It was also at this time that his name became known in Japan.

After achieving resounding success during his five years at the Bastille Opera, Chung suddenly found himself facing an insurmountable challenge. Like his predecessor Barenboim, Chung fell victim to the political maneuvering of the orchestra's administrative management and was forced to resign, contrary to his personal desire as well as that of the Bastille musicians. He still considers this controversy to be the most difficult period of his life. "Having to part with the Opera and the orchestra members whom

I had grown so fond of was more painful than any personal loss of honor," he said.

Six years after his departure from the Bastille Opera, Chung was able to make a triumphant return to Paris in 2000, as permanent conductor for the Radio France Orchestra, one of France's iconic orchestras. The orchestra members as well as citizens of Paris, who knew that he had bowed out in 1994 due to political circumstances, warmly welcomed Chung.

Chung was active in Europe, serving as musical director of Italy's Santa Cecilia Orchestra, when he was invited to Japan, where he was offered the position of special artistic adviser for the Tokyo Philharmonic Orchestra. Founded in Nagoya in 1911, the orchestra moved to Tokyo in 1938, and is the oldest orchestra in Japan. In 2001, it merged with the Japan Shinsei Symphony Orchestra and became the resident orchestra of the Tokyo National Opera House.

Saburo Kurematsu, who had headed the Japan Shinsei Symphony Orchestra before the merger, and Norio Oga, former chairman of Sony Corporation, made earnest appeals for Chung's acceptance on various occasions. Naomoto Okayama, vice chairman of the Association of Japanese Symphony Orchestras, stated: "Before Chung Myung-whun accepted this position, the hard-to-please Japanese classical music fans were nonchalant about attending concerts. But since Chung agreed to lead the Tokyo Philharmonic, there has been such fervor among concertgoers that every concert he conducted has been sold out. With every performance, his reputation has been enhanced not only among music critics but regular concertgoers as well." The fact that his concerts continue to sell out despite a long stagnation due to the recent economic slump is considered quite a remarkable feat in the Japanese cultural world.

Although the Tokyo Philharmonic may have a longer history, the NHK Philharmonic enjoys a superior standing within Japan. Chung, who has conducted both orchestras, has said, "In terms of musical level, the NHK Philharmonic is a step up." Why did Chung then agree to work with the Tokyo Philharmonic, and why are Japanese music lovers now so wildly enthusiastic about the Tokyo Philharmonic?

The manager in charge of audience interpretation at the Tokyo Philharmonic puts it this way: "There is a direct and fervent passion in the music of Chung Myung-whun, which the Japanese people cannot easily find elsewhere. The Tokyo Philharmonic has performed with some of the world's most distinguished conductors, but when they perform with Chung even the air feels different. The orchestra members become more confident and more emotional. The maestro has an exceptional ability to reach deep down inside the orchestra members and draw out the emotions hidden there."

Chung was initially hesitant to accept the post because of his already tight schedule in Europe and also the delicate relationship between Korea and Japan, but he is now pleased with his choice. "Since my youth I have traveled to many lands and performed and conducted in numerous places," he said. "Each time, in each country, I could clearly sense the 'local flavor,' the tastes of the people. The very moment I lift the baton, however, all regional characteristics become meaningless. It is the same with the Tokyo Philharmonic. In that moment there are no Japanese, no Koreans. There is only music."

In March 2003, Chung received the Classical Music Victory Award for his services to the Radio France Orchestra. It was the second time he won the annual award presented to the most active musician in France. The first was in 1995 while he was leading the Bastille Opera Orchestra.

Anna S. Roh Senior Editor, Auditorium **Lee Eun-joo** Photographer

Paik Kun-woo (Kun Woo Paik)

Breathing New Life into Classical Works

If anyone asks me who I think is Korea's most accomplished pianist, I would immediately say, "Paik Kun-woo." Paik is even more well-known and beloved than his wife, one of Korea's favorite actresses. In recent years, he has been recording the complete piano sonatas of Beethoven for Decca, a leading international label based near London, of which two albums have been released.

Paik Kun-woo (Kun Woo Paik) was born in 1946 in Seoul and began learning the piano at the age of eight. He grew up in a musical household, his father playing the violin and his mother the organ. His father insisted that to master an art such as music, one needed to know all about the East and the West. In 1961, Paik left Korea for the United States, where he attended an arts high school in New York and then Juilliard School of Music. In 1965, he debuted at the Carnegie Hall in New York, performing Sergei Rachmaninoff's "Piano Concerto No. 3." Paik gained distinction by garnering the top honors at the Leventritt International Competition and Walter Naumburg International Piano Competition, as well as the Busoni International Piano Competition in 1969.

Three years later, at age 26, Paik made his mark on the classical music scene by performing the complete works of the French composer Maurice Ravel (1875–1937) at Alice Tully Hall in New York. A music critic was so impressed that he commented: "Not even the famous Ravel specialists, French pianist and composer Robert Casadesus (1899–1972) or German pianist Walter Gieseking (1895–1956), have taken on such a challenge. But the young pianist Paik Kun-woo took the risk and had great success. From beginning to end, his performance was skillful and exquisite." In 1995, he performed Ravel's complete works back home in Korea, in a more than three-hour-long concert.

Since 1972, Paik has focused on performing the complete works of composers such as Erik Satie, Claude Debussy, Francis Poulenc, Modest Mussorgsky, Sergei Prokofiev, Franz Liszt, Béla Bartók, Wolfgang Amadeus Mozart, Franz Schubert, Alexander Scriabin, Olivier Messiaen, and most recently, Ludwig van Beethoven. His total commitment and dedication to "complete works" have been sustained through today, earning him the nickname "*Gudoja*," meaning a "truth seeker."

After settling in Paris in 1974, Paik performed Ravel's piano concerto at the Théâtre des Champs-Élysées. Thereafter, he refrained from making concert appearances and worked on broadening his repertoire. Then, in 1991, he

resumed his recording career, with a renewed confidence and refined style.

Paik's dedication to the complete works of composers would not have been possible without painstaking efforts. In 1982, he planned to perform a six-concert series in Paris that would feature 50 works of Liszt. For this, over the next four years, he collected all of Liszt's works and read dozens of books about the composer. Enhanced by his personal understanding and appreciation of the essence of Liszt, Paik's insightful performances struck a resonant chord with the audience, although the repertoire was difficult for general listeners to appreciate.

Paik believes that his role as a concert musician is to draw the audience closer to music so that it can be better understood and appreciated in a new light. He wants his audience to know that classical music is not old and dusty, but can be new and fresh. He says that the true beauty of many works has yet to be uncovered.

Currently, Paik serves as artistic director of the Festival de Musique de Dinard-Côte d'Emeraude, which is held at the coastal resort of Dinard in Bretagne, northwestern France. The festival was founded by Stefan Boutte, a for-

Paik believes that his role as a concert musician is to draw the audience closer to music so that it can be better understood and appreciated in a new light. He wants his audience to know that classical music is not old and dusty, but can be new and fresh.

mer resident of Dinard and a classical music lover, who was such an ardent fan of Paik that he would fly to the United States solely to attend his concert. Paik became involved with the festival when Boutte invited him to perform at the festival in its early years.

In 1994, when Boutte suddenly died at the age of 34, his family and the festival organizing committee asked Paik to serve as the festival's artistic director. "At first, I hesitated because I didn't know how I could fit traveling all the way to Dinard into my busy schedule. But I eventually took the post because it was offered by my friend's family. Planning the festival every year, coming up with a theme, and selecting suitable performers is as creative and enjoyable as giving a recital," Paik explained. Thanks to Paik and the dedicated efforts of the six-member organizing committee, this small-scale event has since grown into one of Europe's most highly regarded music festivals.

After signing an exclusive contract with Decca, an affiliate of the influential Universal Music Group, Paik completed his first Decca recording in June 2000, a collection of piano works composed by Johann Sebastian Bach and arranged by Ferruccio Busoni. Thereafter, he has also released albums featuring the works of Gabriel Fauré, Chopin and Beethoven. "I'm glad I recorded Beethoven at a time when I was fully immersed in his works," Paik said. He thinks of Beethoven as a romanticist, rather than a classicist. Franz Joseph Haydn and Mozart lived a clas-

sicist lifestyle and remained loyal to the royal court. But Paik points out that Beethoven took his music out to the streets. In performing his music for the common people, Beethoven was a revolutionary who sought to reform the social class system. Romanticism was primarily rooted in people and nature, but Beethoven's music was centered around himself and people.

Paik believes Beethoven was a highly passionate individual. Though he never succeeded, Beethoven would repeatedly fall in and out of love. He had a prideful character and would vent his resentment of the elite class, even while aspiring for its acceptance of him. Beethoven's zealous nature and hearing disability made his music all the more extraordinary.

"Beethoven had a fiery temperament. His mindset was resolute and uncompromising. He would go from one extreme to another. But what is so incredible about him was his total dedication to his music, no matter how minor or insignificant a piece might be. That is Beethoven's irresistible attraction," Paik said.

In December 2007, Paik presented an eight-concert series in Korea that featured all 32 of Beethoven's piano sonatas. While striving to breathe new life into the musical genius of Beethoven, Paik Kun-woo, the truth seeker, continues his journey toward enlightenment, guided by a sense of dedication and self-fulfillment.

Jake T. Ryu Editor-in-Chief, Auditorium

Jo Su-mi (Sumi Jo)

Diva with a Voice from Heaven

Jo Su-mi first met Herbert von Karajan in the winter of 1986. After hearing Jo sing, Karajan could hardly contain his amazement. When he asked where she had learned to sing, Jo said that she had studied at the National Academy of Santa Cecilia in Rome. Then Karajan asked where she had studied before that.

"I told him Seoul, Korea," Jo recalled. "This surprised him even more. My basic skills were first honed under my teacher Yoo Byung-moo of Sunhwa Arts High School, and Professor Lee Kyung-sook of Seoul National University. And for this, I will always be grateful to them."

Jo was a second-year music student at Seoul National University when she took off for Italy in the early 1980s, a period of political turmoil in Korea. At the time she was searching for something new. She completed the five-year course at the National Academy of Santa Cecilia in two years and went on to win the grand prize at the Arena di Verona concours and a number of other competitions.

Karajan praised her for having "a voice from above" and one that is heard "maybe once in a hundred years." As conductor of the Berlin Philharmonic Orchestra, Karajan cast a broad shadow over the classical music scene, such that Jo found herself rising quickly to the top follow-ing his discovery of her. In 1987, when Karajan placed Jo on the stage in Verdi's "Un Ballo in Maschera" (A Masked Ball), along with Placido Domingo and the Vienna Philharmonic Orchestra, Jo's name became known throughout the world from the recording of this performance. Though Karajan passed away shortly thereafter in 1989, Jo went on to perform on all the top-flight stages of the world, including the Teatro alla Scala in Milan (1988), Metropolitan Opera in New York (1989), Covent Garden in London (1991), and Bastille Opera in Paris (1993).

Jo returned home in 1988 to perform at the commemorative concert for the Seoul Olympics and was received with thunderous applause from her fellow Koreans, who took much pride in her fame as a world-renowned soprano. In 1994, the year when North Korean leader Kim Il-sung died and the summer is remembered for being one of the hottest ever, Jo returned again to perform a repertoire of Korean songs at the Seoul Arts Center, which confirmed her standing as Korea's "national soprano." By the mid-1990s, when she was acclaimed as "the world's No. 1 soprano," Jo seemed to have nowhere higher to go and nothing more to desire.

At the dawn of the new millennium, Jo was gaining

Soprano Jo Su-mi performs with Italian tenor Andrea Bocelli.

even more widespread popularity in her homeland. A Korean TV station aired a documentary on her success story, and her first crossover album "Only Love" sold almost a million copies. She performed at many international events, such as a cultural festival for the 2000 Sydney Olympics and the Nobel Prize awards ceremony. She also performed with pop singers and appeared with North Korea's Chosun National Orchestra when it gave a performance in Seoul. Even people who were not fans of classical music came to appreciate Jo's world-class talent when she sang the theme song for a popular TV drama series and the 2002 FIFA World Cup theme song.

"I have been trained in classical music since I was born. I don't have much time to spare for pop songs. There are so many new fields to challenge and so many things to learn... I can understand why busy people today don't listen to classical music. So, I have a sense of mission, to attract them to the classical side," Jo says. "My overall goal is to develop my musicality and technique and build up an extensive repertoire. Many artists remain satisfied with what they have achieved and lose the potential to develop further. It is my dream to be constantly pursuing something new but always remain a humble artist."

Any journalist who has interviewed Jo knows that she is friendly, vivacious and open-minded. She likes to joke around, and has a talent for making the conversation interesting as well as insightful. There are few people whose words can be written down as said and come across as natural. Jo is one of these few. In fact, she is one of those rare musicians who also can speak and write well.

"My overall goal is to develop my musicality and technique and build up an extensive repertoire. Many artists remain satisfied with what they have achieved and lose the potential to develop further. It is my dream to be constantly pursuing something new but always remain a humble artist."

"I have tried pop music and musicals, and many different things so that I can cover a wide variety of music. I find Russian and Baroque songs the most difficult to deal with. My major, of course, is bel canto, and in concerts and recitals I have performed French and German songs, including the works of Mozart, but the Russian and Baroque works are the ones I really want to do," Jo says.

Jo is fluent in Italian, French and English, and has a working knowledge of Spanish and German. She says this is natural since she sings in these languages. And in order to sing Russian songs, she has learned Russian as well. The final question of this brief interview was what in particular she had learned from the maestros like Karajan.

Jo replied, "I have worked closely with the maestros, practicing, joking around with them, and also seeing them make mistakes and get upset. But they all had in common a purity of mind. Even now when I think of their eyes, what I see is an untainted mind devoid of calculating thoughts or social niceties. They all knew nothing but music. I learned from them that this kind of purity of mind is what will move the hearts of audiences. I hope that younger singers will remember this too."

If all lived to be 70, would everyone's life be of the same length? Some would say, "Of course, since time is absolute," while others would contend, "The span of your life depends on how you live it." In this regard, it must be said that the divinely talented singer Jo Su-mi is living her life to the fullest, for which I sincerely applaud her.

Park Jung-jun Editor-in-Chief, Auditorium   **Kim Yun-bae** Photographer

Hong Hei-kyung

Prima Donna of the Metropolitan Opera

V erona, Italy, on the evening of Saturday, July 26, 2003. The sun's setting provided little relief to the sold-out audience packed into the open-air arena, where Giacomo Puccini's opera "Turandot" was being performed. The cast included Jose Cura as Prince Calaf, Giovanna Casolla as Princess Turandot, and Hong Hei-kyung as Liu, the ill-fated chambermaid who loved Prince Calaf. At the Arena di Verona, where the performers sing without the aid of microphones, Hong's superb performance was marked by her extraordinary clarity, resonance and vocalization, which enthralled everyone in the arena.

During the curtain calls, the audience saved their most rousing applause for Hong rather than the lead characters. When Liu realizes that her love for Prince Calaf is doomed due to their different social classes, she commits suicide. This poignant scene, highlighted by Hong's passionate performance, left the audience deeply saddened over Liu's tragic fate. Italy's knowledgeable opera fans, who were well aware of Hong's stellar reputation, did not leave disappointed.

I was able to meet Hong in her dressing room at 1 a.m., about one hour after the opera ended. We continued our conversation at a café near the Arena di Verona. Hong's commanding stature, due partly to her notable height — she stands as tall as or even taller than most Western opera performers — as well as her open-hearted personality and dignified manner, is part of what makes her one of the most impressive Korean women on the global stage.

Hong talked first about the importance of her family life. She told me a story about when she received an invitation to perform Verdi's "La Traviata" at the Arena di Verona Opera Festival in 2004. Although she had been eager to perform the repertory of "La Traviata," she felt hesitant to accept the invitation because the festival was scheduled for the summer, which was the only time she could spend with her family. Hong has achieved success as a prima donna and enjoyed a happy family life by balancing the demands of her professional career with her personal priorities. Her family values were readily evident from our conversation; she ended up declining the Verona offer at the time.

Hong has said that she learned how to sing before she knew how to talk. With a natural vocal talent, Hong went to the United States while she was a middle-school student. After receiving a full scholarship to the Juilliard

Hong performs with tenor Placido Domingo in Mozart's opera "Idomeneo."

At the Arena di Verona, where the performers sing without the aid of microphones, Hong's superb performance was marked by her extraordinary clarity, resonance and vocalization, which enthralled everyone in the arena.

School of Music at the age of only 16, she went on to perform in many operas while studying at this prestigious institution. Winning the top honors at the Metropolitan Opera Auditions in 1982, she made her debut on the stage of the Metropolitan Opera House in New York in 1984, in Mozart's opera "La Clemenza di Tito" (The Celemency of Titus), conducted by James Levine. Over the next 17 years, Hong has become one of the most beloved performers at the Metropolitan Opera, landing lead roles on a regular basis.

Hong has starred in a number of notable operas, playing such roles as Ilia in "Idomeneo," in which she shared the stage with Placido Domingo; Pamina in "Die Zauberflöte" (The Magic Flute), which was performed to commemorate the 200th anniversary of Mozart's death; the Countess Almaviva and Susanna in "Le Nozze di Figaro" (The Marriage of Figaro); Juliet in "Roméo et Juliette"; Mimi in "La Bohème"; Micaëla in "Carmen"; Gilda in "Rigoletto," together with Luciano Pavarotti; Liu in "Turandot"; and Zerlina in "Don Giovanni."

In addition to this impressive resume of opera performances, Hong has also appeared with the world's leading orchestras. These have included performances of Brahms' "Requiem" and Mahler's "Symphony No. 4 in G Major," which she performed with the Los Angeles Philharmonic Orchestra led by Andre Previn, as well as a rendition of Carl Orff's "Carmina Burana," which she performed with the Met's James Levine.

Hong has also released noteworthy recordings on global markets. For example, her aria album, produced in collaboration with the Saint Luke Orchestra, gained instant popularity, and so did an album of opera duets, "Bel Canto," in which she is featured along with mezzo soprano Jennifer Larmore. What's more, she has also released an opera album of her Julieta role from a performance of "I Capuletie I Montecchi," composed by Vincenzo Bellini, and produced an album in Paris of Korean songs as a collaborative effort with the Orchestral Ensemble of Paris, conducted by Kim Duck-ki.

For anybody interested in experiencing Hong's performances on European stages, I would recommend a DVD album that includes several of her most outstanding operatic performances. Hong's consummate talent is well demonstrated in her rendition of the role of Musetta in "La Boheme" staged at La Scala in Milan. This particular opera was directed by Franco Zeffirelli and conducted by Bruno Bartoletti. Watching her passionately perform the role of the vibrant Musetta, as she shares the stage with tenor Marcelo Alvarez and baritone Roberto Serville, I am overwhelmed by a sense of pride in Hong's boundless artistry.

Chang Il-bum Music Critic **Lee Eun-joo** Photographer

Chang Han-na
From *Wunderkind* to Master Cellist

There are few spheres of human endeavor that are so deeply enamored with *wunderkind* (wonder child) as classical music. Over the last 20 years, Korea has produced a number of musical child prodigies whose remarkable talents have been internationally recognized. But most of these brilliant young musicians achieved their fame abroad before being properly acknowledged in Korea.

Such is the story of cellist Chang Han-na. She emerged as an international wunderkind in 1994 when she won both the grand prize and the contemporary music prize at an international cello competition presided over by Mstislav Rostropovich. She was the youngest winner in history, a record that still stands. Compared with violin or piano, the cello is an instrument rarely mastered by young performers. After this contest, cello legends Rostropovich and Mischa Maisky both volunteered to mentor Chang. Rostropovich was notorious for his reluctance to take young talent under his wing, so his offer created quite a stir in the classical music world.

Rostropovich and Maisky were not the only maestros to be captivated by Chang's talent. Her performances impressed two prominent conductors, the late Giuseppe Sinopoli and the New York Philharmonic's resident conductor Lorin Maazel; both have maintained close relations with her, helping to advance her career.

It was only after her victory in the Rostropovich competition that Chang Han-na became known in her homeland, Korea. When the media reported that she had to struggle during the competition because of the mediocre quality of her instrument, the Korean Business Council for the Arts presented her a priceless Guadagnini cello, made in 1757. Thereafter, she has distinguished herself as a young Korean genius of classical music, alongside violinist Sarah Chang, two years her senior, who had made her mark at a somewhat earlier age. These two Chang girls turned 20 in 2001 and 2003, respectively, and have since established themselves as adult musicians who have outgrown their wunderkind label.

Although they were active in similar realms — the United States and the EMI record label — their musical pathways and personalities, which had seemed quite similar early on, began to reveal marked differences. Unlike Sarah, who had chosen to concentrate wholly on music by enrolling at the Juilliard School of Music, Han-na surprised everyone when she entered Harvard University last

"The humanities provide rich nourishment for the human heart, and music is an art for expressing people's innermost sentiments. By reading Goethe and being inspired by Tolstoy, I hope that my music may become as rich and mature as their works."

year to major in philosophy.

"The humanities provide rich nourishment for the human heart, and music is an art for expressing people's innermost sentiments. By reading Goethe and being inspired by Tolstoy, I hope that my music may become as rich and mature as their works." That is how Chang explained her chosen path in 2002 when she returned briefly to Korea to give a recital. She was carrying a copy of Nietzsche's "Thus Spake Zarathustra" in her hands, rather than sheet music. To combine university study with concert performances is no doubt highly demanding, but her grades are reported to be excellent.

Unfortunately, Korean audiences have had few opportunities to enjoy Chang's live performances. Spending most of her time in Europe and the United States, she has returned to Korea only once every one or two years. Korean audiences thirsting for her music have thus had to content themselves with her recordings. Ever since her wunderkind days, she has maintained an exclusive contract with EMI, which has led to the release of "The Saint-Saens Cello Concertos," conducted by Rostropovich, "Haydn Cello Concertos," conducted by Sinopoli, and "The Swan," a collection of short pieces.

Recently, Chang has created yet another sensation with her fourth album, "Prokofiev: Sinfonia Concertante/Sonata for Cello and Piano," which she recorded with the London Symphony Orchestra, conducted by Antonio Pappano. Released in February 2003, the album was recognized as the best concerto recording of 2003 in both the Gramophone Award bestowed by the U.K.'s authoritative classical music magazine Gramophone and the Echo Classic Award from the German Recording Association. In January 2004, the album also topped the list of the "soloist plus orchestra" category of France's Cannes Classical Awards.

Presented for the 10th time this year, the Cannes Classical Awards are based on a poll of some 700 critics from eight countries, including Germany, the U.K. and the United States. Along with the Diapason Award, it is one of the most prestigious French awards for recorded music. In the U.S. market, the same recording has been nominated for a Grammy Award. With classical music preferences having subtle differences in the U.K., France, Germany and the United States, in order for a recording to receive awards in all four countries there must be a universal quality that is evident to all such audiences. A spokesperson for EMI said, "Because each country has distinct preferences in classical music styles, no previous recording has captured awards in all four countries."

Those who are acquainted with Chang's conscientious character and zealous work ethic (she is known for practicing endlessly) regard her as a genius type who could have succeeded in any field as impressively as she has as a cellist. When Chang says that she has never thought of herself as a genius, she is not so much being modest as objecting to a failure to give due credit for her tireless dedication. If her father had not bought her a cello when she was four years old, and if she had not fallen in love with the cello upon hearing a performance by Jacqueline du Pré, she says she would have become a heart surgeon.

"The heart is the one organ in the body that must never stop working. I was curious to know how surgeons could operate on the heart with a scalpel," said Chang. Today, she wields a bow instead of a scalpel, in a concert hall instead of an operating room. Inasmuch as her music enables the hearts of her audience to beat on, in a sense has she not achieved the same result?

Anna S. Roh Senior Editor, Auditorium   **Lee Eun-joo** Photographer

Kang Hyo

Teacher of Young Korean Musicians

The International Sejong Soloists is a multinational chamber ensemble founded in Seoul in 1995. It gives regular concerts in New York, among other activities abroad.

The Great Mountains International Music Festival & School is held annually in Gangwon-do Province in August, the hottest time of the year in Korea. Because of this, any mention of summer automatically causes me to think of Kang Hyo, artistic director of this notable event. Every year when I see Kang, I would greet him by saying: "Your Korean has improved." In response, Kang, a kind of low-key person, would pause, often for as long as 10 seconds, before saying anything. He contemplates and smiles with a hint of bemusement, and then instead of answering he asks: "Do you think so?"

The relative slowness of his Korean is evidence of just how long Kang has been away from his homeland. Born in 1945, Kang first left for America in 1964, while a student at Seoul National University, so he has now been living abroad for more than 40 years. In the United States, he studied at the Juilliard School and the Peabody Conservatory of Music, and then returned to Juilliard as a graduate student and later became an instructor at its Pre-College Division. In 1985, the Juilliard School of Music appointed him a full professor and he has since taught such young violinists as Sarah Chang, Gil Shaham and Chee-Yun.

So, how hard might Kang have been working all this while? Kim Gyeong-jun, who won the violin category of the first GMMFS Concours in 2004, is one of his students. When I asked him how many Korean students he was teaching at Juilliard these days, he said it's about 15. In the field of music, this is no small number. I then recalled something I heard a long time ago: When the Korean National University of Arts was being launched, there was a rumor that Kang Hyo would be appointed a professor at Seoul National University. In the end, however, he did not return to Korea.

"I have no regrets. It has been very rewarding to teach

Korean students overseas," Kang said. "I can do much more for my homeland by being at Juilliard. The biggest advantage is that I can personally support talented students when they come to study in the U.S. I was also able to attract world-class musicians to the GMMFS because I was in America."

The faculty of the GMMFS is truly remarkable. Moreover, they are all musicians of Kang's "people network." This is an indication of how ardently he has immersed himself in the world of music during his past four decades in the United States. This is also why Korean corporations, planning to hold some "mega-events" abroad, invariably seek out Kang's assistance. His close relationship with Samsung, the sponsor of the International Sejong Soloists (host ensemble of the GMMFS), is a good example. The apple of Kang's eye, the International Sejong Soloists has been giving regular concerts in New York since May 2005, when the group celebrated its 10th anniversary. Every Thursday, visitors to "Samsung Experience" on the third floor of the Time Warner Center in New York are treated to a free performance by this chamber ensemble.

Kang's busy schedule gets more hectic as he has to travel constantly back and forth between Korea and the United States. I inquired about whether he had any regrets about cutting short his career as a concert musician. To this, he laughed aloud, waved his hands, and said, "No"

Then, he added: "Of course, at first I was mainly a performer. But with time, I began to teach, then I split my time between performing and teaching, and the amount of time spent teaching gradually increased. I had even become a person responsible for the International Sejong Soloists — before I realized it. Now I spend all my time and energy on education."

For 30 years, beginning in 1969, Kang was a member of the Kennedy Center's permanent chamber orchestra in Washington, D.C., performing alongside contemporary masters. The artistic director at the time was pianist Leon Fleisher who, due to numbness in his right hand, had begun to focus on conducting. "I really learned a lot when Leon Fleisher was the artistic director," Kang said, recalling those early days. Kang said that when he was in his twenties, he quickly learned from every performance, and therefore he dearly values the experiences of his youth.

He said, "Your feelings from your childhood last a lifetime. It seems I haven't forgotten a single thing from my childhood. When I chat with my friends all my old memories seem to come alive again. Once, as we were passing by Daehan Theater, one of my friends said: 'Didn't

The third Great Mountains International Music Festival & School in 2006, hosted by the International Sejong Soloists, held a charity concert for flood victims at Naksansa Temple.

you have a concert here?' I replied: 'It was summer then, too.' When the Juilliard String Quartet first performed at the auditorium of Ewha Womans University, the time that I traveled from Daegu to Busan because I heard the legendary black alto Marian Anderson was having a performance there… all these memories are still fresh in my mind."

It was natural for Kang, who so dearly cherishes the memories of his youth, to assume the duties of artistic director of the Great Mountains International Music Festival & School. Learning music and relaxing in nature for musical appreciation and development — this is already the trend of music festivals worldwide. The scenic mountains of Gangwon-do Province in summer offer an ideal venue for musicians as well as music fans.

The Great Mountains International Music Festival & School provides diverse programs based on a new theme each year. Audiences can enjoy a wide variety of music with no particular genre or period dominating. Huge outdoor screens are set up at Yongpyong Resort, the site of the music festival, to attract guests of the resort and neighborhood residents to the performances, where even ragged T-shirts and flip-flops are welcome attire.

"When I was young, I loved snow so much. I found delight in the smallest of things. As time goes by we become less sensitive to small things around us. Life turns gradually somber and we lose our joy. But when we hear beautiful music and our hearts open up, we feel that the world has changed. The sky looks bluer, the air feels clearer, and people seem kinder. It feels like we can do anything. You have had these feelings, haven't you?"

No doubt this is because music has mysterious powers to turn the world around 180 degrees and make us happy, as Kang says.

Park Yong-wan Reporter, Auditorium   **Kim Yun-bae** Photographer

"I can do much more for my homeland by being at Juilliard. The biggest advantage is that I can personally support talented students when they come to study in the U.S. I was also able to attract world-class musicians to the Great Mountains International Music Festival & School because I was in America."

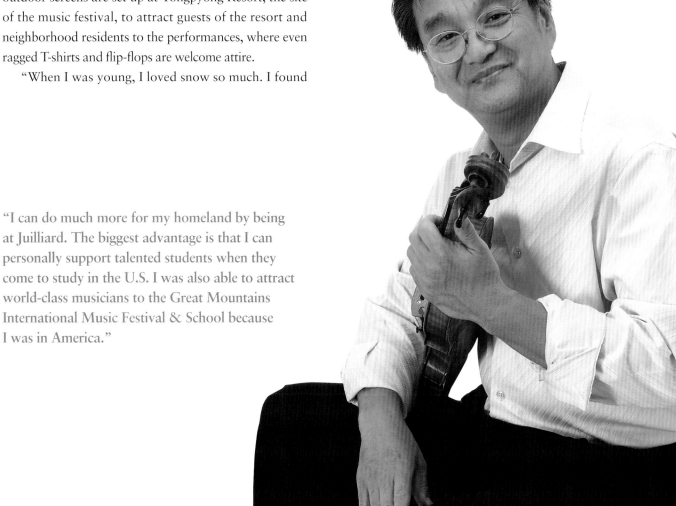

Chin Un-suk (Unsuk Chin)

Composer at the Vanguard of Contemporary Music

Since she left Korea more than 20 years ago, Chin Un-suk (Unsuk Chin) has ardently pursued her passion for music and made her way to the fore-front of contemporary music in Berlin. In 2004, she achieved great popularity in her motherland, Korea, when she was named a recipient of the Grawemeyer Award. Established by Charles Grawemeyer, the award is presented to contemporary music composers who are recognized as world leaders in their respective fields. Chin does not appear to be disappointed at all about having had to wait all this while to gain recognition in Korea, nor does she seem overly impressed with the welcome mat being laid out for her these days. Chin has always gone about her work quietly and in her own way, paying little heed to matters unrelated to her music. Nevertheless, Korea's music community has taken enormous pride in her success abroad.

After receiving the Grawemeyer Award, which many regard as a "Nobel Prize" of the contemporary music industry, Chin returned to Korea for the first time in four years, in the spring of 2005, to serve as resident composer for the Tongyeong International Music Festival. Upon her arrival, Chin mania soon engulfed the nation's music circles. In 2006, she was appointed composer-in-residence for the Seoul Philharmonic Orchestra. And she was again in the spotlight in June 2007, when her opera "Alice in Wonderland" was premiered in Munich. There is no doubt that Chin's successful achievements have steadily upgraded the global standing of contemporary Korean music. Chin has also created a groundswell of interest in contemporary music; "Alice in Wonderland" has served to open the eyes of the public to the fact that new operas are actually being composed and performed in the 21st century.

I remember that in the 1990s, when I had little personal knowledge of Chin, I thought she was a kind of "extraordinary lady." After all, how else could this individual, who had to overcome the formidable obstacles of being a woman in the male-dominated music world, and one from Asia at that, become one of the most respected figures in the field of contemporary music? However, I also imagined that this woman, as awe-inspiring as her struggle to reach the top might have been, must be "aggressive" if she was able to attain such notable success. Moreover, I assumed, much like the style of music she composes, her personality could probably be complex or

"The trend toward composing music for easy listening has spread throughout the world. I personally believe that this is not an entirely desirable development. Although the public might applaud and enjoy such music produced mainly for commercial purposes, such works are usually forgotten within a year or two. And the reasons such pieces became popular in the first place also soon disappear."

even difficult to understand.

But since the dawn of a new century, there has been an "evolution" in my perceptions of Chin. Above all, I finally had the opportunity to listen to her music in person. This was in 1991, when her work "Akrostichon-Wortspiel" (Acrostic-Wordplay) was first performed in Amsterdam, as part of the festivities to celebrate her victory at the prestigious Gaudeamus Concours. It was performed by the Nieuw Ensemble, a group that specializes in contemporary music. The piece has since been performed in some 15 countries under the baton of such preeminent conductors as George Benjamin, Simon Rattle and Kent Nagano. In this way, "Akrostichon-Wortspiel" has served to greatly enhance Chin's international reputation. Of course, all of this was possible because of the world-class quality of her composition. For me, the music was so deeply moving that any reservations that I might have had toward Chin simply vanished.

After receiving the Gaudeamus International Composers Award in 1985, while she was in her mid-20s, Chin remembers how she was brimming with confidence as she headed for a critical meeting with György Ligeti, perhaps the greatest composer of the 20th century, who she hoped would accept her as his student. However, she found herself crashing down when Ligeti pointedly told Chin that she needed to "talk in your own language, not in that of others." Chin remembers feeling immense pressure whenever this maestro gazed at her with his piercing eyes. When Ligeti retired from the Hamburg Music Academy in 1988, many of his students, who regarded the opportunity to learn from him as the very reason for their existence, felt like they had been cast adrift without a captain.

This was true of Chin as well. She moved to Berlin, where she hoped to sort things out. It took about three years before Chin returned to her music, and heeding Ligeti's advice to "talk in your own language," she composed "Akrostichon-Wortspiel."

Chin recalled: "I did not compose any music for three years, and in effect did nothing more than age by that many years. I really had a hard time. I think my reward for this hardship was the attainment of spiritual enlightenment. I really did not do anything. I just existed in a constant state of depression. Finally, I could not do that anymore even if I wanted to. I still find myself being overcome by depression whenever I finish a composition. However, I am now a professional, not a student. Nowadays, I keep being asked to write music or to work on certain projects. Therefore, I can't live so extravagantly as I did back then."

In June, the premiere of "Alice in Wonderland" was performed by the Bavarian State Opera. Chin, who once said that "I do not want to abuse such a wonderful story for my own musical advancement," adapted a parody of the 19th century Victorian tale as the storyline of her work. Chin's second opera "Through the Looking-Glass and What Alice Found There" is scheduled to open at the same theater in 2013. Whereas "Alice in Wonderland" revolves around a card game, "Through the Looking-Glass and What Alice Found There" has a more complex plot centered around a game of chess. These days, contemporary music is apparently geared to "easy listening." On the surface, Chin's music seems to be in conformance with this trend. So, what are the thoughts of Chin, one of the composers at the forefront of mainstream contemporary music, about this phenomenon?

The spotlight was focused on the composer, Chin Un-suk, when the opera "Alice in Wonderland" was premiered at the Bavarian State Opera in Munich in June 2007.

"I'm against any form of shallow music," she said. "I think the ideal type of music must satisfy two conditions: when music professionals hear it, they should be able to find something special about it, and for the general audience, it should strike an emotional chord. For a few years, there has been a fad that focuses solely on the pursuit of new trends. But such a pedantic approach can create a sense of alienation between contemporary music and its audience. The current situation stands in complete contrast. The trend toward composing music for easy listening has spread throughout the world. I personally believe that this is not an entirely desirable development. Although the public might applaud and enjoy such music produced mainly for commercial purposes, such works are usually forgotten within a year or two. And the reasons such pieces became popular in the first place also soon disappear."

When I asked Chin what she was most concerned about these days, she said that she was worried about finding out what direction she should take in the future. To me, this seemed to be an ephemeral response, like trying to catch a passing cloud. Then again, don't we all have the same worries as Chin about yesterday, today and tomorrow? Chin also told me about the twists and turns in her life, like needing three attempts before being admitted to Seoul National University's Department of Composition, never receiving financial support from her family, and being so elated with receiving the Grawemeyer Award that made her feel like the winner of a big-money lottery. It seems that such difficulties along the way have made her hard-earned success that much sweeter. For me, and other music lovers in Korea, one sweet thing to do should be wonder about when Chin Un-suk will compose and present a work that is the "future."

Park Yong-wan Reporter, Auditorium   **Wilfried Hösl** Photographer

Shin Joong-hyun

Living Chronicle of Korean Rock Music

"The father of music" is a title generally given to classical composers such as Bach. Whereas Germany has Bach, the maestro of classical music, Korea has Shin Joong-hyun, the god-father of Korean rock. It is no easy matter to reach the top in any field, let alone for a popular musician to earn the designation "maestro," a distinction usually reserved for the classical genre. In Korea, however, no one would object to conferring this title on Shin. Such an honor would help to break down the prejudiced view of classical music as lofty and popular music as vulgar, and to set Shin in his rightful place in the world of Korean music.

Shin planted the seed of Korean rock music, introducing rock to the country in the 1960s when the very genre was virtually unknown. This caused a great stir in the world of Korean popular music, which at that time was dominated by Japanese-style "trot" songs. In 1962, Shin formed Korea's first rock band, Add 4, and released the country's first original rock record, "Woman in the Rain." This provided a model for the Korean-style adaptation of rock music. What is particularly remarkable is that as Shin continued to release rock records into the 1970s, he always kept pace with the best bands from the birthplace of rock music, the United Kingdom.

"It's a big mistake to see Korean rock music as a mere imitation of Western rock," Shin said. "Like all music, rock is a universal language. What's important is to put something of your own culture into the international style of rock. If you just imitate foreign music, you end up producing a rootless culture. Whether it is rock, jazz, or rap, Korean music should have a Korean flavor."

Shin's songs are full of Korean feeling. Although he plays the guitar, when listening to his music you may be reminded of the traditional Korean zither *gayageum*, or the traditional vocal form *pansori*. This is perhaps the most distinctive feature of Shin's music. His experimental drive to create a uniquely Korean rock music is clearly illustrated by his 1970 recording, "Beautiful Woman." The introduction to "Beautiful Woman" is remarkable for its descending line, la-so-mi-re-do, borrowed from the pentatonic Korean scale *gung-sang-gak-chi-u*, which leaves out the fa and si of the Western seven-note scale. The melody, too, echoes that of the cheerful Joseon period (1392–1910) songs, *taryeong*. The accompaniment is played on a guitar, but evokes the tone of the gayageum. In the lyrics, the line "Everyone loves her, I too love her"

It is no easy matter to reach the top in any field, let alone for a popular musician to earn the designation "maestro," a distinction usually reserved for the classical genre. In Korea, however, no one would object to conferring this title on Shin Joong-hyun.

(*modu sarang-hane nado sarang-hane*) suggests the rhythms of pansori. Shin's efforts to perfect the Korean-style rock music do not end there. In his search for a truly Korean rock-and-roll sound, he has even modified his electric guitar.

"In today's Korean music scene, there are many attempts to graft traditional and Western music together. But the public response has so far been tepid. It is no simple task to blend musical styles that have been formed in different cultural environments," Shin says.

From this point of view, Shin deserves high praise for his ability to impart a Korean flavor to his music without losing the true essence of rock.

To be ahead of your time is not to follow every superficial fad. Perhaps this is why the public, though sensitive to new streams, turns away from anything that bears a label like "avant-garde" or "experimental." This is what happened to Shin's early work. His band had a real cutting-edge sound for Korea at the time, and his lyrics were fresh in their understated restraint. But he was too far ahead of his time to make a big hit from the beginning, and Korea's first rock band, Add 4, broke up after just three years.

Instead of giving up, Shin made a new effort to establish a Korean group sound. He pioneered a unique sound combining the rock-and-roll beat with traditional Korean rhythms. After Add 4, he formed a series of bands — Jokers, Donkeys, Questions, The Men, Shin Joong-hyun and the Coins, and most recently, Kim Sakkat — but they all pursued a single goal: to perfect a distinctly Korean style of rock music.

Another important characteristic of Shin's music is that it retains the authenticity of traditional music without losing the contemporary sound. This can be seen from the way his songs of the 1970s and 1980s are constantly being revived by younger singers. His music does not seem at all old-fashioned today, even to young listeners. The fact that his music can remain popular through changing times is the result of his determined efforts to create truly original music.

Together with this up-to-date sensibility, another quality that should not be omitted from any discussion of Shin's music is the deep resonance that sets it apart from other rock music. This resonance is Shin's artistic spirit pouring out from within. When he wants to express sadness, for example, he does not try to grasp the intense emotion of the moment when sadness is at its peak, but instead focuses on the feeling that lingers on when one has no tears left to shed. The deep resonance that rings in his music stems from this reflective restraint. Perhaps this is why he insists that the true nature of rock does not lie in "letting yourself go."

Shin goes on, "There is a big difference between making noise and turning noise into music. What matters is not letting yourself go but finding your inner resonance. It is a question of restraint and moderation. Even when relying on tradition, we must not lose the contemporary feeling; even the avant- garde must be human."

This helps to explain why of all the different instruments, he has stuck to playing just the guitar. Not only can the electric guitar interface with computers and machines, but Shin considers it the only instrument capable of raising noise to the level of music.

For 40 years, Shin has devoted himself solely to rock music. In all that time, he has never turned aside from his chosen path. He has lived only for his music, and found happiness in making music alone. Why has he always clung so tenaciously to rock music? What charm does he find in it?

Shin is immersed in thought in his workroom.

"To me, rock is the genre that can embody life with the most frank and uninhibited expression. From rock, I learned that even noise and dissonance can be music. Rock is surely the most vibrant and immediate form of music."

Shin has been called "a living chronicle of Korean rock music." This can also be seen in the all-embracing scope of his musical activities. He has written both the lyrics and music of over 300 songs, and has been dubbed "the Jimi Hendrix of Korea" for his masterful guitar playing. He is both a vocalist and a talent scout with a knack for discovering promising young singers. Although he has not often sung his own songs on the stage, his husky voice, at times melancholy, at times murmuring sarcastically, remains in the hearts of his fans.

Shin's life has not been one of constant sunshine, however. On the contrary, the light in his life has been brief and the darkness long. In the 1970s, just as rock music had finally managed to enter the mainstream, it suffered a hard frost on the grounds of its supposed hedonism and immorality. Associated with hippie resistance to the patriarchal order and the defiant spirit of the blue-jeans culture, rock music was suppressed by the Park Chung-hee regime, which had seized power in a coup d'état. Not only rock musicians but folk singers, who formed another major genre of popular music in the 1970s, were branded as "marijuana-smoking entertainers" and arrested in large numbers. Shin was one of the victims. On the grounds that his songs were hedonistic, his singing style vulgar, and his lyrics liable to fuel social and political unrest, 100 of Shin's songs were banned, and Shin had to step down from the stage at the height of his career.

Shin turned his frustration into a new opportunity. Thereafter, he paid less attention to harmony than to the depth of his voice and the spirituality of his music. At this time, he became deeply interested in Oriental philosophy. This enabled him to produce his much-discussed albums of the 1990s, "Nature at Rest" and "Kim Sakkat," in which the traditional instrumental solo genre *sanjo* is transferred to the electric guitar. These albums owe much to the nature-friendly philosophy of Laozi and Zhuangzi, who believed in the unity of nature and man. Indeed, many of Shin's 300 songs deal with nature themes. He once remarked in an interview: "If I could be one with nature, I would wish for nothing more." But what is the essence of the music he pursues?

Shin says: "It's not a problem of instruments, but of musicality. If you become too attached to harmony, you

1 "Body & Feel," an album released in 2002.
2 Shin at Woodstock with his guitar.

lose the true essence of music. Music without artistry is nothing more than noise. Music must have an inner depth that produces sound and moves the heart by human effort. Only then will there be a true harmony of sounds between human voice and instrument. The important thing is to keep the middle path without leaning to either side, and to build up your inner strength. If your own world doesn't waver, you can express your whole musical life with a single guitar string, or even with a single note."

The place where Shin has been standing during his 40-year musical career is not under a spotlight on a gaudy stage.

"I prefer the small theater to the TV studio, the shade to the sunlight. The few times I have appeared on TV, I felt that I had become a showman, somehow artificial or insincere. And so I made myself a promise: Rock is an art for the people. As long as there is even one person who appreciates my music, I will not refuse to perform, no matter how small the venue is."

Shin has kept his promise to this day. Perhaps it is this steadfast faith that has made him a maestro.

Shin's name has often been attached to the words "the first," and another "first" came in 1997 when a group of young singers made a splash with an album entitled "A Tribute to Shin Joong-hyun," the first Korean tribute album in honor of a living musician. But Shin is not content to be called "the first." Rather, he seems immersed in building a legend that will be "the longest." This can be seen in his latest album, "Body & Feel," in which he looks back over his musical career at the age of 65. What makes this album special is that he not only wrote all of the lyrics, music and arrangements, but handled the whole production process himself and even sang most of the songs. And in September 2002, he began a six-month series of twice-monthly free concerts that will continue until March 15, 2003, at his own performance venue, Woodstock.

"The reason I keep performing live is that I believe music should be real music that lives and breathes with people face-to-face. And the reason I keep playing the guitar is that I want to break down the prejudice that lumps all rock together as noisy, hedonistic music. There is an urgent need to create a cultural climate in which rock can be properly appreciated."

Shin dreams of a rock revival. He has no fear of old age. Probably, we must say, "Old soldiers never fade away" rather than "Old soldiers never die, they just fade away." When I asked, "How long will you go on performing on stage?" he answered without hesitation, "Until I die."

This inscrutable statement reveals the secret of a maestro who has turned himself into an extraordinary medium and instrument.

Yoo Meoung-jong Poet　**Choi Hang-young** Photographer

2

Architects

Joh Sung-yong

Architecture Aspiring for Harmony with Life

In terms of world architecture, Korea is a country still hidden away. Though little known to the rest of the world, Korean architecture has a rich and unique tradition. The main hall at Jongmyo, the royal ancestral shrine of the Joseon Dynasty (1392–1910) in Seoul, has been inscribed on the UNESCO World Heritage List. Several other wooden works from the Joseon period are also counted among the masterpieces of Asian architecture. They include Changdeok Palace, where the buildings and landscape complement each other subtly and beautifully with little trace of artifice, and Gyeongbok Palace, which is an architectural manifestation of Confucian ideology.

What, then, is the case of contemporary Korean architecture?

If anything, Korea's contemporary architecture is even less known than its traditional architecture. Buildings that have made a mark on the architectural scene have largely been constructed in a handful of European countries, in the United States and Japan. Korean architects have made few buildings that have drawn the notice of the architectural world.

The accomplishments and potential of Korean architecture began to be recognized, however, with the construction of Seonyudo Park, a small island park hidden away in a quiet corner along the banks of the Han, Korea's largest river, which cuts through the city of Seoul. The park features no large impressive building, which is what most people expect of "architecture," nor an artistic building boasting a creative new aesthetic. It has no dazzling attractions or exotic natural setting. In size it is also nothing extraordinary. But from the moment it took shape it grabbed the attention of architects and landscapers around the world who saw it as a new and inspired work that expanded the concept of parks.

The park site is an island formerly used as a water purification plant. When the plant fell into disuse the city

Seonyudo is the work that best reveals Joh Sung-yong's architectural philosophy and design talents.

of Seoul decided to turn the island into a public park. The design that was selected through a competition did not stipulate removal of the old facilities and creation of a park on top of cleared ground. Rather, it called for reworking of the old structures and their incorporation into the overall scheme as well as utilization of parts of the old water facilities as sculptural elements in the park. The park was designed to embody the values of environmental preservation and recycling. Like the abandoned power plant that became the Tate Gallery in London, and the disused railway station that became the Musee D'Orsay in Paris, an old water purification plant was reborn as the centerpiece of an ecological park in Seoul.

At the park the old building containing the pump room was transformed into the Hangang River Museum, the ceilings removed to leave only the pillars standing like sculptures entwined and encircled by plants. The integra-

tion of old concrete structures into the garden creates a mood of unusual beauty that is hard to find elsewhere in the city. Visitors are treated to a new experience of nature, architecture and the recycling of resources. In living up to this purpose, Seonyudo Park was a success from the beginning. The park was instantly popular with locals and foreign visitors alike when it opened in 2002, and it is now purposely sought out by architecture students and architects from other countries when they visit Seoul.

The man who created Seonyudo Park is Joh Sung-yong. His buildings are acclaimed for their harmonious assimilation into the natural environment, how they seem to grow out of the land and become an extension of it. Seonyudo is the work that best reveals his architectural philosophy and design talents.

In Korea, Joh is an architect who is both famous and not famous. If asked to name the country's leading archi-

1

2

tect, most Koreans would name someone else. Joh has not designed many famous big buildings and is not widely known among the general public. But if the same question were posed to the country's architects the answer would be quite different. His influence is paramount among younger architects and he has always played a central role in bringing new issues and discourses into the open. He is the architect most admired by his peers and the one who has always made a social issue of Korean architecture and acted on his beliefs. When he was assigned commissioner for the Korean pavilion at the 2006 Venice Biennale, he also helped to promote Korean architecture to the world.

The work that made Joh's name known was a large apartment complex, the athlete's village for the 1986 Asian Games in Seoul. The Asian Games are a big international event and could be called the Asian Olympics. The 10th edition of the games, held in Seoul, was the first major international event to be hosted by Korea since going through the great tragedy of the Korean War in 1950 and overcoming the scars of the war to achieve economic growth. Given the great commission of designing the athlete's village at the age of 42, young for an architect, Joh created an apartment complex in a park setting, which made him famous in domestic architecture circles.

The Asian Games athlete's village saw the germination of concepts that would form the core of Joh's later work: harmony of buildings and landscape, architecture of social significance, and going with the flow of nature. Joh may be an architect but he is quick to say that architecture is, in the end, not art — that is, architecture is not an artistic endeavor where the creator freely pursues his or her own ideals, but the task of rationally creating a space that meets certain conditions and systems. While the resulting work can sometimes achieve the lofty reaches of art, it is

Joh's architecture is neither grand nor showy but this is what enables them to blend in so beautifully with nature and the city. Joh is therefore the architect who best finds contemporary expression for the Korean people's traditional aesthetic that flows like water, who shows both the universality and distinction of contemporary architecture.

Joh's view that art is not the basic premise of architecture.

Furthermore, Joh does not mold his buildings like sculptures. He emphasizes the importance not of each individual building but the whole that they create when they are together. The assemblage of buildings in Seoul is different from that in Chicago, for example, and as such an assemblage holds great significance.

Based on such a philosophy, it is natural that Joh seeks architecture of social significance and that his greatest interest is in finding his role as an architect in society. He is not convinced that it is the work of architects to build a lot of grand structures, as he believes the relationship between architecture and the city, and the city and human beings, is more important than the building itself.

This philosophy was first revealed clearly in the student union building at Inha University (1985), located in Incheon, Korea's third largest city. Given the job of redesigning the existing building, Joh came up with a structure that has no main entrance but many entrances that people can use to enter the building from any chosen point.

What was the reasoning behind such a design? The student union building houses a variety of functions including a post office, the school newspaper and broadcasting station, stores and student club offices. There may be one building but many different types of people entering the building for many different purposes. This is the point Joh considered to be most important. He saw the building as a small city. As there can be no single entrance to a city the student union building caters to various paths of circulation. Joh believed that creating a convenient, democratic building was more important than building one that just looked good on the outside.

Joh's architectural philosophy of harmony between the built structure and its natural setting is best manifested in the Uijae Museum of Korean Art (2001) located near the southern city of Gwangju. Nestled on the slope of Mt. Mudeung, the symbol of Gwangju, the museum is a small building made of wood and glass. Its strong point is the way it seems to form a part of the landscape rather than sticking out to dominate it. It is so highly acclaimed that one critic even said Korean museum architecture can be divided into the periods before Uijae Museum and after Uijae Museum.

The success of Uijae Museum did not come from the brilliant design alone. Joh, who had fallen into a slump at the time, traveled the 400-kilometer distance from his home in Seoul to the construction site more than 140 times over a period of three years. The actual construction being as important as the design, Joh poured his body and soul into supervising and managing the work to ensure the quality of the finished building. Uijae Museum is thus the result of much devoted effort.

The museum is also the building that best manifests the concept of "*punggyeong*" (landscape) that is a keyword in Joh's architecture. Joh's idea of punggyeong, however, is a little different from the English word "landscape." It is an all-inclusive word that speaks not of a beautiful view but of the mood and feeling at the point of contact between humans and a particular place. It is a concept that expresses a particular point in time enhanced by emotion and memory. Hence Joh explains his own architecture as "revealing the landscape." He sees his role as putting a new perspective on a landscape and investing it with new meaning by placing a building in it.

Aside from Uijae Museum, Joh has designed several other art museums including the Soma Museum of Art at Olympic Park in Seoul and Zien Art Space in the outskirts of the city. Zien Art Space in particular represents Joh's reso-

Soma Museum of Art at Olympic Park in Seoul.

lution of the concept of landscape in architecture and shows the beauty that can result from experiments in this line.

Zien consists of several small buildings clustered together as in a village. It is not built on top of the land. Rather the land was dug out so the museum could be built into the slope with its roof at a similar height as the surrounding hills. From above it appears that the land and the building are at the same level, flowing without interruption. Joh calls this kind of design a "roofscape."

As Joh seeks to create buildings that have social significance and harmonize with their surrounding environment rather than being striking in themselves, photography does not do justice to his works. Only by seeing the buildings firsthand in their natural setting does the easy beauty

of these creations become apparent. The road and nature are naturally drawn into the building, going through and continuing unbroken to the outside again, which means visitors can walk through the building as if walking through a forest.

In the end Joh's architecture is neither grand nor showy but this is what enables them to blend in so beautifully with nature and the city. Joh is therefore the architect who best finds contemporary expression for the Korean people's traditional aesthetic that flows like water, who shows both the universality and distinction of contemporary architecture.

Goo Bon-joon Journalist   **Ahn Hong-beom** Photographer

Seung Hyo-sang

Recreating the Tradition of Korean Architecture

If Antonio Gaudi y Cornet's Sagrada Familia Cathedral in Barcelona had been built in a Korean city center, would it have been as impressive? No. Only when architecture is in harmony with its surroundings does it truly come to life. That is to say, whatever is built in Korea should be Korean in style. A Korean architect who holds firmly to this principle is Seung Hyo-sang, president of Iroje Architects & Planners.

Asked point-blank, "What is Korean architecture?" he replies without hesitation: "Western architects try to fill space. We try to empty it." As a telling example, he cites the yard. A Western courtyard or garden serves as a foil to the building, while the Korean *madang* is an independent space with a natural life of its own. He adds that Korean architecture lays little stress on the separate functions of different living spaces. Whereas the rooms of a Western house are named after their function (living room, bedroom, bathroom), Korean rooms are designated only by position: inner room (*anbang*) or opposite room (*geonneon bang*). "Function," Seung insists, "was virtually ignored in traditional Korean architecture. You can see that best of all in the empty madang. The yard was an open space that might just as well be used for a feast as for a funeral."

Historically, the Korean yard was quite unlike the Western or Japanese garden. It was used for all kinds of social gatherings, but it was also a place for pacing in solitary meditation. At other times it was an undefined space whose significance lay precisely in its emptiness. But there was another place that showed the special flavor of Korean architecture: the open hall, *daecheong maru*, which provided both shade and breeze in the sultry summer. Glossing over the boundary between inside and out, the hall expressed the Korean sense of harmony with nature.

So there is something very Korean about Seung Hyo-sang's architectural urge to empty a space rather than fill it up. But at first glance, his buildings have a strong feeling of Western modernism, probably due to their minimalist lines and heavy use of concrete. In this he has often been compared to Japanese architect Tadao Ando, but the analogy doesn't seem to please him. "There may be some similarity in form, but the aesthetic behind it is totally different," Seung says. An architect's work is bound to be infused with his ideas and Seung's ideas bear a thick streak of folk tradition.

Seung has inherited the idea of the yard as an empty

space like the voids in an Asian painting, where emptiness produces its own kind of repletion. But he also draws on another inheritance, as a lineal successor to the two great figures of modern Korean architecture, Kim Chung-up and Kim Swoo-geun. In particular, he acknowledges his intellectual debt to Kim Swoo-geun as the teacher who imparted to him the whole sensibility of an architect. At Kim's Space Group of Korea, a mecca for Korean contemporary architects, Seung learned "the architect's eye, his stance and even his responsibility to society." He venerated Kim as a teacher of life as well as art and an incarnation of Korean architecture.

The two first met in 1971 when Seung enrolled in the Department of Architecture at Seoul National University.

As soon as he graduated, he apprenticed under Kim at the Space Group of Korea, where he remained until 1986. During those 15 long years Kim was his only textbook. But when Kim died in 1986, Seung had to close the covers of that well-thumbed book and the next few years were years of struggle. He felt compelled to transcend his teacher's legacy and find his own creativity and originality.

Seung began to achieve self-sufficiency in 1986 when he founded his own architectural study center, Iroje. Before long he was designing superb buildings bearing his own unique stamp, such as the Nulwon Building (Busan, 1989), Seongbuk-dong House (Seongbuk-dong, Seoul, 1990) and Sujoldang (Hak-dong, Seoul, 1992). His talents were recognized with the Korean Institute of Archi-

Sujoldang House in Seoul, designed in 1992.

Seung Hyo-sang is fond of borrowing architectural motifs from Korean tradition for his compositions in bare concrete. As a result, he brings out the plain and robust quality of the unfinished that lies behind the architectural concepts of his ancestors.

tects Award (1991 and 1992), the fourth Kim Swoo-geun Architecture Prize (1993), and most recently, an invitation to the Venice Biennale.

Seung is fond of borrowing architectural motifs from Korean tradition for his compositions in bare concrete. As a result, he brings out the plain and robust quality of the unfinished that lies behind the architectural concepts of his ancestors. "From olden days," he comments, "Korean builders have seen a wall as nothing more than a boundary between inside and out, with no need for excessive decoration. In a house with too much adornment, it's hard to see the inhabitants. Architecture is not for decoration, it's for people." If traditional Korean architecture could realize the spirit of abstinence even in the walls of a building, Seung feels bound to do the same.

In 1996, Seung laid out his architectural philosophy systematically in a book. *The Aesthetics of Poverty* is sure to be mentioned whenever his name comes up. Its title, he explains, does not mean that we should live in poverty, but that we should have the wisdom to be content with less.

Seung explains: "Poor people don't knock down buildings in a hurry. When they need more space, they either add onto an existing building or they increase the amount of shared space at the expense of private space. The aesthetics of poverty is all about conservation and sharing."

He firmly believes that this aesthetic of poverty was embraced by the Korean literati of old, who shunned displays of wealth and made their homes embody a philosophy of abstinence and emptiness.

Besides expressing tradition in modern form, Seung lays great stress on achieving harmony between humans and nature. This aspect of his work can be clearly seen in his current project at Paju Book City. As coordinator of this unusual 100 percent architect-designed development, he has mandated roads that restrict the traffic speed to 20 kilometers per hour, buildings no taller than 15 meters

and strict conservation of the existing hills, streams and reed beds. In short, he is aiming for a green city. An essential part of his architectural philosophy is that just as a building can only come to life when it is in harmony with its surroundings, people, too, must not lose their ties with nature. "Architecture that preserves the natural environment upholds the value of sharing. When high-rise buildings hide the hills and forests, they deprive people of the right to share the beauty of nature," he says.

"As an architect," Seung once remarked, "I would name three outstanding pieces of cultural heritage in Korea. The Jongmyo Royal Ancestral Shrine teaches us about our roots. The humble yard epitomizes the architecture of our lives. And the Demilitarized Zone stands as a doleful monument of our times."

National Treasure No. 227, the Jongmyo Royal Ancestral Shrine, where the memorial tablets of the Joseon Dynasty kings and queens are kept, was added to the UNESCO World Heritage List in 1995 for its significance in maintaining a five-century tradition of Confucian memorial rites. But that is not what matters to Seung. Paying little attention to the stylistic and historical aspects of the building, Seung has his own reasons for considering it an emblem of Korean architecture.

"Jongmyo expresses the Korean view of death, namely that the souls of the dead do not disappear but interact continually with the land of the living. That's why this austere 117-meter-long rectangular building not only embodies the essence of Korean architecture, but has the power to plunge us living souls into a long and reverent silence. It is both an immortal work of architecture in which form and content are fused as one, and an eternal hometown that gratifies the instinctive Korean desire to return from whence we came. Naturally, Jongmyo also shows the Korean architectural aesthetic of emptiness, for its core is a spacious yard."

Seung strives to incorporate into his own designs the Korean architectural prototypes that he finds in old buildings with urban-style spatial configurations, such as the Buddhist temple Seonamsa and the Confucian academy Byeongsan Seowon. But when he turns to the present, his main feeling is sorrow. He finds it undeniable that the rigorous spirit of his ancestors, who imbued every building with a deep philosophy, has been sorely tarnished by their successors. Perhaps this is why he names the Demilitarized Zone, with its half century of untouched natural ecology, as a cultural heritage. "Four kilometers wide and 248 kilometers long, the DMZ's 1,000 square kilometers

of natural wilderness is the only part of Korea that has escaped the rush of development," he says. Although it is the product of a tragic era, he implies that our own best legacy is what we have left alone.

How will he design buildings in the future? His reply is terse: "Before asking how, we should think hard about why." He probably means that by focusing only on methods we lapse into an architecture circumscribed by technology. He earnestly believes that architecture can change the shape of human life. Accordingly, he argues: "A true architect asks himself how he can use space to guide the lives of the people living inside."

Currently, Seung is preparing for an exhibition by building a little city. Named the Artist of the Year by the National Museum of Contemporary Art Korea, he has been allocated a generous space within the museum building in Gwacheon for a large-scale display showing how architecture affects our lives. The "Aesthetics of Poverty Exhibition" will run for two months from August 28, offering much insight into the work of Seung Hyo-sang.

In the midst of his busy schedule of preparations for this year's exhibition and his work as coordinator of Paju Book City, Seung recently received some welcome news. On May 11, he was awarded honorary membership in the American Institute of Architects. At the award ceremony in Charlotte, North Carolina, he remarked: "Above and beyond the individual honor, I hope this will become an occasion for Korean architecture to transcend its parochial condition and become known to the world." His unique architectural aesthetic with its modern application of traditional principles had at last won international recognition. The award must have been all the more meaningful to Seung since in 1985 it had been bestowed on his teacher, Kim Swoo-geun.

From early September, Seung will also be showing his work at the Venice Biennale, where he will represent Korea in an exhibition entitled "Chinese Literary Culture and Architecture," featuring architects from four countries that traditionally shared that culture: China, Korea, Japan and Vietnam. "It will be a good opportunity," says Seung, "to restore the beauty of traditional Korean architecture that has been distorted by the influx of modern ideas from abroad, and to display it in a storybook setting. With European architects getting more interested in East Asian styles, it will also be a perfect chance to show them what we've got."

Choi Tae-won Freelance Writer   **Choi Hang-young** Photographer

Hwang Doo-jin

Korea's Hope for "Seoul-like" Architecture

Gahoeheon is a new restaurant that the Wood & Brick, one of the oldest Italian restaurants in Seoul, opened in Bukchon, a traditional residential area in Seoul.

To Western eyes the traditional architectures of Korea, China and Japan may look much the same. Some aspects are certainly very similar: the tiled roofs that are delicate and somehow heavy at the same time, the spatial composition of small structures joined together, the design and the black and brown color scheme resulting from the use of wood and earth. Sometimes it is indeed hard to distinguish the architecture of one country from another, and foreigners can hardly be blamed for thinking they are all the same.

But each country's traditional architecture is unique. To the Koreans, Chinese and Japanese their respective architectures differ even more than the Gothic style from the Romanesque. They can tell straightaway a building's provenance. Koreans see Chinese architecture as highly decorative and Japanese architecture as simple, composed of straight lines. In contrast, Korean architecture is characterized by softly curved lines, and its spatial arrangement and landscaping also differ greatly from what are found in China and Japan. These differences are more clearly apparent in ordinary homes rather than grand structures such as palaces and fortresses.

The architectures of the three countries differ even more in engineering than in style. Though the same can be said of any country in any region, traditional architecture results from deciding what is most suitable and economical for the climate and environment. All over the world, traditional architecture is the product of hundreds of years of experimentation with materials that are easily available and simple to handle in building structures that most effectively deal with the weather.

Unlike countries in the West, Korea has no large deposits of sandstone with which to construct grand buildings of stone, and unlike China has no soil suitable for making bricks. The materials available in Korea are wood, yellow soil (loess) and granite. Because of the extremes of hot summers and cold winters, Korean houses were made to accommodate both: the *ondol*, an under-floor heating system, provided warmth in winter, and the *maru*, an open wooden-floored hall that allowed ventilation between the different structures of a house, kept the house cool in summer.

The ondol and maru are thus the two key elements of a traditional Korean house. The ondol, in particular, is a uniquely Korean concept, completely different from the Western fireplace or any other heating system of eastern Asia. Stones were laid underneath earthen floors and heat from a furnace was channeled through flues underneath, creating radiant heat that lasted for a long time.

The generic name for traditional Korean houses is *hanok*. Pulling together the cultural DNA and science and technology of the Korean people, hanok are the pride and essence of Korean culture. After surviving over thousands of years, in the 20th century traditional housing faced the challenges of rapid modernization and subsequent Westernization. As concrete buildings became the global standard, sweeping away traditional architectures around the world, hanok too were pushed aside in favor of new Western-style buildings. The traditional house became a

Hanok in Bukchon – Jibwunheon House in Gahoe-dong, Seoul

He knew of no university in Korea which had studied its neighborhood. This changed his approach to architecture. From a small town in America he was able to take a step back and look at Seoul more closely. When he returned to Korea in 2000, he set up his own company and took his first steps toward becoming a "neighborhood architect."

special genre, surviving mainly as designated cultural treasures or in special institutions such as temples.

While hanok seemed in danger of disappearing in the late 20th century, interest in them is now reviving in the 21st century. Contemporary Korean architecture has adopted the hanok, transforming and developing it into a new genre. While not actually building traditional houses, architects sought to incorporate selected features of traditional housing into modern buildings. But these days they are experimenting with ways to preserve the distinctive quality of hanok intact while developing them as living spaces for contemporary Koreans.

One of the architects leading this movement is Hwang Doo-jin. Early on in his career Hwang introduced the hanok as an important element in his architecture, as seen in a series of works in the heart of Seoul. At the same time he wrote books and articles arguing for the revival of hanok, thus playing a large role in bringing traditional housing into the center of architectural discourse.

Architecture is said to be an art that blossoms with

maturity. Time gives the architect greater social perception, knowledge and experience, which form the ground for the creation of a good building. Hence it is not unusual for architects to be active in their 60s when everyone else is retiring, and even into their 70s. For an architect the 40s may be the time one's identity as an artist is taking definite shape. Adopting traditional architecture as contemporary architecture, Hwang, who is only in his 40s, is one of the Korean architects most in the limelight.

Hwang's perspective differs from the 20th-century Korean architects who saw hanok as pre-modern architecture at the end of its life, or as part of the cultural heritage that had to be outgrown. He believes in the evolution of hanok into contemporary architecture. He believes that as the housing type best suited to the Korean climate, hanok can be adapted to the needs of contemporary life and once again become widespread as a form of architecture. Being made primarily of wood, most parts of a traditional house can be reused, which makes them environment-friendly. From a socio-economic perspective, Hwang asserts that hanok must become more common.

In his urban housing Hwang has amply demonstrated the evolutionary potential of hanok. Though working with the same elements, he has employed them in different ways. He is not a slave to the principles of traditional housing, but has pursued changes according to situation and conditions. Among his works in Bukchon, the oldest authentic hanok village surviving in Seoul, some appear to be a replica of the traditional style while others are so contemporary that even Koreans wonder whether they can be called hanok at all.

The most renowned of Hwang's works is Gahoeheon, a traditional house clothed in contemporary architecture to create a highly distinctive structure. It is an Italian restaurant with glass walls merged with hanok to create a new kind of space with a special atmosphere. In contrast, other works such as Chwijukdang (House of Jade Bamboo) and Ssanghuijae (House of Double Happiness) so faithfully succeed the hanok tradition that they seem little different from any other traditional house. The interiors however are snugly functional, satisfying the demands of Koreans today. Hwang's hanok draw an enthusiastic response because they have a clean sophistication without being radical.

However, Hwang does not call himself a "hanok architect." He simply employs traditional housing in his creation of contemporary architecture. He defines his architectural theory as doing his own thing without following any particular style. What he would call himself is a "neighborhood architect."

The neighborhood is the smallest residential unit in the city. Hwang takes his own neighborhood as both the departure point and destination of his work and through it investigates the relationship between human beings and the environment, between architecture and society. He believes architects should look for issues in their immediate surroundings and find ways to deal with them through architecture. Rather than clinging to big values and themes, the architect should first solve concrete problems that have been experienced firsthand. "The architect should know his neighborhood better than anyone else. It's important to manifest good thoughts and wisdom in the neighborhood and share them with people outside the neighborhood," Hwang said. "In that way the architect should continuously expand his neighborhood, from the neighborhood to the city, from the city to the whole country."

Armed with this critical consciousness, Hwang chose the neighborhood in which he now lives. Tongui-dong is a place in the heart of the city which, different from other neighborhoods, retains historical and cultural traditions but is also relatively static. After settling down there Hwang began to investigate the history of the area and at the same time started to hone his architecture by creating new buildings for the neighborhood. Most of his major recent works are actually concentrated within a radius of 2-3 kilometers from his home.

Hwang realized the importance of the neighborhood concept while studying for a master's degree at Yale University in the United States. He was surprised to find that the lectures and research concentrated on the town of New Haven where the university is located. He knew of no university in Korea which had studied its neighborhood. This changed his approach to architecture. From a small town in America he was able to take a step back and look at Seoul more closely. When he returned to Korea in 2000, he set up his own company and took his first steps toward becoming a "neighborhood architect."

Therefore, before giving any grand definition of architecture and aiming to be the country's leading architect, Hwang believes it is more important to become the best architect in his own neighborhood. Gradually the confines of the neighborhood can be expanded. One of the things he hates most is indeterminate internationalism. Among the ranks of "neighborhood architects," he counts two of the most famous architects of today: Tadao Ando (1941–) from Japan and Rem Koolhaas (1944–) from the Netherlands. Like these two masters, Hwang wants his architecture to reach fruition in his own neighborhood before advancing into the wider world.

While studying his own neighborhood, Hwang is also carving out his own architectural identity through various activities other than architecture. As a complex art, architecture overlaps with many other fields but in reality few architects have much exchange with artists in other disciplines. Hwang is perhaps the most active Korean architect when it comes to collaborations in other fields. He has designed an exhibition space for a photographer and taken part in a performance art project. With a great interest in all areas of design, he has produced interesting pieces ranging from a necktie to a table. His unique "Kao Rocking Chair," a modern reworking of the rocking chair concept, has been purchased by the National Museum of Contemporary Art Korea.

Through such wide-ranging activities Hwang is training himself in pursuit of the ultimate goal of making the most suitable architecture for his hometown of Seoul, of finding the architecture that is the most "Seoul-like." In the process of rapid development and expansion the architecture of the city has yet to show any Seoul-like universality or distinctiveness. Born and bred in Seoul, Hwang is now planning to expand his neighborhood to the whole city. Certainly he is still young, which means he has loads of potential. The domestic architecture circle is hoping that Hwang's creations will be able to enhance the face of this vast city, Seoul.

Goo Bon-joon Journalist **Ahn Hong-beom** Photographer

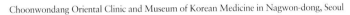

Choonwondang Oriental Clinic and Museum of Korean Medicine in Nagwon-dong, Seoul

Film Artists

Lee Chang-dong
Realist Chasing the Invisible Light

When people want to introduce Korea and Korean society to foreigners, the movies they first recommend are those made by Lee Chang-dong. To get a feel for the sentiment of traditional society, Lim Kwon-taek's "Sopyonje" is a good choice, and for a taste of the new creativity and changing face of Korea today, Bong Jun-ho's "The Host" (*Gwoemul*) or Park Chan-wook's "Sympathy for Mr. Vengeance" (*Boksuneun naui geot*) may be ideal. But for a more concrete idea of what has been happening in Korea and what sort of people make up this society, Lee Chang-dong's movies are the first that come to mind: "Green Fish" (*Chorok Mulgogi*), "Peppermint Candy" (*Bakha Satang*), "Oasis" and "Secret Sunshine" (*Miryang*). These movies are works of art that honestly show Korea and its people with indelible imagery.

Interestingly, Lee was a novelist with a brilliant career before he started making movies. He made his debut through an annual literary competition in 1983 when he was a high school Korean language teacher. He made his name as a realist, winning the Isang Literary Award in 1987 and the Hankook Ilbo Literary Award in 1992. His first foray into filmmaking was in 1993 as assistant director of "To the Starry Island" (*Geu Seome Gagosipda*) and made his directorial debut in 1997 with "Green Fish." In 2002, "Oasis" won the Director's Award at the Cannes Film Festival and in 2007, Jeon Do-yeon won the Best Actress Award for "Secret Sunshine" at Cannes as well. Recognized as a powerful figure both in literary and film circles, Lee was appointed the minister of culture in 2003.

Both as a novelist and filmmaker, Lee has always been interested in the details of history and real life. He delves into questions such as where this place in which we are now living is headed, and where this distorted time and space of ours originated. He throws out these questions to the audience, making them think about how they should see the figures on the screen and how they should understand them.

Lee's debut film, "Green Fish," is set in the new satellite towns of Seoul where life is rapidly changing. It explores the identity of Korean youth and the changing nature of places in Korea. Mak-dong, an ordinary country boy before he comes to Seoul and joins a gang, gains wealth but loses so much more — his friends, family, his girlfriend Sun-su, his past, and his very self. This movie casts a cold eye on the youth of Korea who are crash-

Lee does not directly show us what that invisible light is, but leads us indirectly how to find it. It's this aspect that makes us realize why Lee is a great director. Lee depicts not abstract figures but the reality of Korean life and society today. He depicts it in its heartbreaking entirety.

ing about and hurting themselves as the country hurtles toward modernization and globalization.

Lee makes movies from the realist's perspective. Some movies are like a kaleidoscope providing an escape from reality; and then there are movies that reflect our lives and society as they are. "For me, movies are about reality," says Lee. "They should show not only what's on the surface but also what's hidden underneath." In this light, Lee's second work, "Peppermint Candy" is special to Koreans, for it depicts Korea's tired modern history in all its true gruesomeness.

Time runs backward in "Peppermint Candy." We are introduced to Yeong-ho as the president of a small business living a depraved life, and as a brutal police detective who catches and tortures students fighting for democracy. Then we go back in time. We see Yeong-ho as a young policeman who still believes it is his job to protect the citizens, and as a young man honestly and madly in love with a woman who doesn't feel the same way. This is not to drum up sympathy for the wrongdoer. As a businessman and a police officer, Yeong-ho is definitely a villain.

At the same time, Yeong-ho is a father and a son. He's not some kind of monster that we find hard to understand but just one of those weak, inconsistent people who can be found anywhere. He is not the personification of evil but the propensity toward evil that exists in all of us. Every one of us has the potential to be that kind of human being if we lose something inside and bow down to evil. By showing the change in Yeong-ho's life Lee explores the idea of "innocence." "I wanted to show that we are losing innocence. What is the innocence of real life? In the simplest terms, it's something like shyness. Everyone's lost their bashfulness these days," says Lee.

If the two movies discussed above explored Korea's

1   "Peppermint Candy" (1999)
2~3 "Oasis" (2002)

modern history, "Oasis" and "Secret Sunshine" are movies about people around us here and now. Gong-ju, the heroine of "Oasis," is disabled and not like everybody else but she has the same love and affection for human beings as anyone. Born with serious cerebral palsy, she speaks with difficulty and to her family she is a bit of a nuisance and an object of sympathy at the same time. She is not their equal, however. And most people think of her the same way.

Jong-du, just out of prison, is also an outsider. He's not the least bit concerned about what others think of him. He does whatever he feels like doing, wherever his heart leads him. There is no cause and effect. He just forges ahead, gets into trouble, and feigns innocence. Though Gong-ju and Jong-du are similar they have lived totally different lives. Jong-du acts with his body, charging ahead into the world without thinking. It's his way of dealing with other

people's contempt. Gong-ju is unable to move freely but she dreams her private dreams, caught in her own world. When the two meet Gong-ju's dream becomes reality and Jong-du's reality becomes one where dreams are possible.

Gong-ju and Jong-du are people who live on the outside of society. Not even on the fringes. We believe such people are not equal to us. We consider the love between an ex-convict and a disabled person to be different from what's normal. It's impossible to even think of the two falling in love and making love because we believe they're not the same as everyone else. While showing us these prejudices, Lee makes no explanations for Gong-ju and Jong-du. As he follows them around and observes their lives, he takes the audience with him and makes them look over his shoulder.

Ex-convicts and the disabled — they are not outsiders but people who live and breathe in the same space as we do. But we have treated them as if they are invisible. Making us conscious of this fact is where the power of "Oasis" lies. As a novelist, Lee says one of his major themes was human dignity, how a person keeps his dignity as a human being. "I wanted to see on what grounds the pitiful ordinary person with no plans or way out justifies his existence," he says.

"Secret Sunshine," which deals with salvation, is divided into three parts. The first part shows Sin-ae, a widow, living with her son in Miryang, a town in southern Korea. Though she says "I'm not unhappy," she looks it. The child longs for his father but Sin-ae is still in a daze. Her husband had already abandoned her before he died, but she still won't acknowledge it. The second part shows Sin-ae caught in despair when her son is kidnapped and killed, and turning to religion for consolation. Without the strength even to cry, Sin-ae happens to attend a church outreach meeting where she finally lets herself go and weeps bitterly. Afterwards she finds peace. She loses herself in religion, believing that her sadness and despair are all part of God's will. But to find real peace she has to forgive her child's killer.

Intending to forgive him face to face, she goes to meet the kidnapper. What she finds is a man who has already been forgiven by God. He repents his past, and has found peace thanks to God's forgiveness. This is where the third part of the movie starts. Sin-ae was going to forgive him anyway, so isn't it a good thing that he's already been forgiven? But it turns out that what Sin-ae really wanted was the satisfaction of forgiving him herself. She wanted to confirm for herself that she had by the grace of God found the strength and peace of mind to forgive her enemy. But everything starts to go wrong.

Anger takes over. How dare the kidnapper sit before her looking so peaceful while she has been living in anguish? She is overcome with hate and starts to assail God. How could God forgive the man who had given her so much pain and promise him heaven? She starts to rebel. She steals, seduces a church elder's husband, and inflicts pain on herself. Through these acts she wants to find out if God is really watching. In this way Sin-ae falls apart.

Giving the story in this fashion is dull perhaps but necessary to understanding the movie. Talking about the images and the theme alone would not give the whole

"Peppermint Candy"

picture, because "Secret Sunshine" is a very literary film. Everything, not only the images on the screen, is connected to everything else. To see what "Secret Sunshine" is all about the viewer needs to concentrate not only on every line of dialogue and every prop, but also the path in which the characters move and their habits and short life histories. The attention to detail is almost suffocating. It's not a world that can be seen with the eyes but one that can only be entered by understanding what one sees.

The movie is not critical of religion. In fact, Lee doggedly insists on dealing with religious salvation and divine or worldly providence. If fate leads a person to despair, nothing can be done to overcome it. One cannot beat it, only endure. There is no end, and running away or lean-

ing on something will not make the despair and pain go away. Herein lies the secret of this world. The Korean title of the movie, "Miryang," is the name of a small town and at the same time a metaphor for "secret intentions."

In the end, God reveals nothing visible. The thing we have to see is something that is not easily seen — the invisible light. In "Secret Sunshine," Lee does not directly show us what that invisible light is, but leads us indirectly how to find it. It's this aspect that makes us realize why Lee is a great director. Lee depicts not abstract figures but the reality of Korean life and society today. He depicts it in its heartbreaking entirety. This is true realism.

Kim Bong-seok Film Critic

Jeon Do-yeon

Actress Draws Passion from the Ordinary

If asked to name the leading film actress in Korea, without hesitation, I would answer, "Jeon Do-yeon." It's not just because of her swag of awards, including all the major film awards in Korea and the Cannes Best Actress Award for her role in "Secret Sunshine" (*Miryang*) in 2007. Jeon's record of distinction is not just a couple of impressive movies; she is a consummate actress who has portrayed the most diverse and most challenging roles in Korean film. Ordinary looking but attractive, provocative yet elegant, gentle yet tough — her image seems to be the archetype of all Korean women. Jeon is therefore Korea's preeminent film actress and the very image of contemporary Korean women.

Jeon's career began in 1990 when she appeared in a television commercial. Parts in TV dramas soon followed, but she was not the lead. It seems she was always cast as the heroine's younger sister or best friend. The reason was clear: her looks. No one would call Jeon Korea's most beautiful actress. So beside the gorgeous heroine she was destined to play the part of the spirited, aggressive friend.

While playing these smaller parts, however, Jeon was quietly learning about her own strengths and weaknesses. She may not have had the charisma to grab attention on the spot but she had a chameleon-like quality that allowed her to shine in diverse roles. So even from those early days she was already developing into the strong character actress she would later become. With no strong individuality of her own, she developed into an actress who could melt into any character.

In 1997, director Jang Yun-hyeon's debut film, "Contact" (*Jeopsok*), a sensitive description of Korean society in the process of change, was released. Those were the days just before the Internet became common. The lead characters in the movie develop a relationship via dial-up PC communications. One scarred by a past relationship and one suffering because of unrequited love, they communicate via computer which allows them to keep their identities hidden. Hence their relationship is not a face-to-face romance that explodes into passion, but a careful, cautious love that grows slowly. The story was a huge hit with young audiences. The lead role, Su-hyeon, initially a rather feeble, dreary kind of person, proves to be an honest character who gradually finds herself. And through this persona the movie star Jeon Do-yeon was born.

Jeon is not a star who relies on her looks. She does not have the kind of charisma that can captivate audiences

just by showing her face on the screen. Instead she moves audiences by digging deep into her character and immersing herself in the role. She may have been no more than a supporting actress on TV but through "Contact" she became a movie star overnight. Her subsequent movies, "The Promise" (*Yaksok*), where she plays a smart doctor who falls in love with a gangster, and "Happy End," showed that Jeon has the talent to become Korea's leading actress.

In "Happy End" Jeon plays Choi Bo-ra, a married woman who runs an English language academy. Choi is a self-assured character who is the breadwinner of the family, instead of her unemployed husband, and who carries on an affair with a younger man. It is a role that showed audiences yet another side of the actress Jeon Do-yeon. The movie was made in 1999, a time when Korea was in upheaval following the financial crisis that hit two years before. Countless men who had lost their jobs were psychologically troubled and women who witnessed the helplessness of men for the first time fought to come up with ways to survive. Society made new demands on women who had to take control of their own lives. But the world had not changed completely. Feeling threatened by women, men lashed back in anger, asserting patriarchal values.

As a working woman Choi has to take care of the children and the housework after coming home from the office. Her husband, powerless after losing the role of family head, plots to regain his authority in the home. Choi, accepting the conflict that she faces, boldly forges ahead and in the process draws a portrait of today's real-life young Korean women. "Happy End" was an early indication of the great diversity of Jeon's range as an actress.

In "Untold Scandal" (*Scandal: Joseon namnyeo sang-*

The women Jeon portrays, even as they agonize over love, do the dishes and the washing every day, and go to work every day in order to make a living. Surely no other actress can wear the uniform of a lowly office worker as if she were born in it. This is where Jeon's real charm lies.

1 "The Promise" (1998)
2 "Happy End" (1999)
3 "Untold Scandal" (2003)

nyeol ji sa) from 2003, a reworking of the French film "Dangerous Liaisons" set in Korea's Joseon period, Jeon appears as the chaste Lady Jeong who ends up being seduced by the greatest womanizer of her time. Under Joseon society's oppressive Confucian ethics, Lady Jeong, a widow, lives a life of chastity. Little by little, however, she is drawn into the world of passion but with tragic consequences. The movie ends neatly with her suicide.

In this movie Jeon portrays a repressed woman whose passions gradually build up and finally explode. It's a very different role from the bold, brash women of "Happy End" and "No Blood, No Tears" (*Pido nunmuldo obsi*). But Jeon was perfect in her new role. A character who wavers between morality and desire and who is unable to choose either one, Lady Jeong epitomizes the plight of Korean women caught in the trap of convention.

It is hard to say what Jeon Do-yeon the actress is really like. If asked to name her best work, most people would answer, "Happy End" or "Secret Sunshine," but neither of these roles can be said to define her oeuvre. While Jeon is undoubtedly a superlative actress, there's another reason for her success over the past 20 years: She is the actress most Korean women can identify with. Jeon is flawless in those scenes where she portrays the kind of woman one could easily run into in the neighborhood. She is entirely convincing as the girl or lady next door.

In "I Wish I Had a Wife Too" Jeon plays Won-ju, an ordinary bank teller. She's not particularly attractive, not

particularly smart, and not particularly good at anything. She's an ordinary woman living a humdrum life but nevertheless, in Jeon's hands Won-ju is a warm and very likable person. She's so familiar that she makes you think of someone you know, or even yourself. The women Jeon portrays, even as they agonize over love, do the dishes and the washing every day, and go to work every day in order to make a living. Surely no other actress can wear the uniform of a lowly office worker as if she were born in it. This is where Jeon's real charm lies.

Jeon plays two roles in the fantasy film "The Little Mermaid" (*Ineo gongju*). Na-yeong works at a bank. Her mother, Yeon-sun, is a tough, aggressive woman who makes a living scrubbing people's backs at a bathhouse. Na-yeong loves her mother but is ashamed of her at the same time. One night, for some inexplicable reason, Na-yeong travels back in time and meets her mother as an innocent young island girl. She's surprised to find that even her mother who is embarrassed by nothing and has not the slightest shred of refinement, was once an inno-

cent young girl as well. She realizes that the lovely girl was sacrificed for the aggressive old woman in order to feed the family. Yeon-sun's transformation reflects the lives of all Korean mothers. Jeon plays both the characters of Na-yeong and the young Yeon-sun artlessly and movingly. When "The Little Mermaid" was released audiences said it was like watching an album of Jeon's acting. It was a movie where Jeon was passionate and at the same time so natural she seemed to be playing herself.

In the 2005 movie, "You Are My Sunshine" (*Neoneun nae unmyeong*), the character Eun-ha is a wonderful vehicle for showing off Jeon's subtle charms. A waitress at an old-style teahouse, Eun-ha has an affair with a simple country boy but later discovers she has contracted AIDS. Though often driven to prostitution to pay the bills, Eun-ha has a happy, bubbly personality, not because she has everything she wants but because that's her natural disposition. She lives a rough and tumble life but she never gives up on herself. She challenges every obstacle that stands in her way. Her battles are not grand wars but little everyday struggles, just like those fought by all Korean women. "The Little Mermaid" and "You Are My Sunshine" help us to realize how tough Korean women are and to understand why they undergo transformation into those brassy matrons we disparagingly call "*ajumma*."

Then there's "Secret Sunshine." No doubt it is the high point of Jeon's acting career. In this movie she showed us her whole arsenal of talent. Playing a woman who loses her precious only child, Jeon moves between the extremes of the calm before the storm and the violence of madness with the skill of one possessed. Though she finds peace after turning to religion she falls into the hell of despair after meeting her son's killer. She despairs in God. She agonizes over God's judgment and salvation. But an ordinary woman, the only thing she can do is descend to madness. Unable to seek revenge against God, she turns to self-destruction. Jeon portrays this process of destruction with unqualified ferocity. That such lunacy can be portrayed from an ordinary-looking exterior is nothing short of amazing.

After "Secret Sunshine," Jeon got married and appeared in "My Dear Enemy" (*Meotjin haru*) where she plays a city girl worn out by everyday life. A character somewhat more chic than the women in "I Wish I had a Wife Too" and "The Little Mermaid," she is still an ordinary kind of person. These ordinary women are portraits of ourselves, representations of Korean women. Jeon is not Korea's leading actress for nothing.

Kim Bong-seok Film Critic

1 "You Are My Sunshine" (2005)
2 "My Dear Enemy" (2008)
3 "Secret Sunshine" (2007)

Hong Sang-soo
Filmmaker Takes Less Traveled Path

Hong Sang-soo is gradually losing his eyesight. While working on "Virgin Stripped Bare by Her Bachelors" (*Oh! Sujeong*), he experienced vision problems for the first time. But he did not concern himself with proper care for his failing eyesight; rather, he abused his eyes. Every time he made a new film, his vision continued to deteriorate. He remained indifferent, saying, "Everyone will eventually lose their vision and pass on." But it does not seem possible for his worsening vision to be overcome by sheer determination alone. Still, he explains, "I'm somehow accustomed to my situation. I can even sense when a problem will arise. Because I can sense its onset, I can also control it, somewhat." It is difficult to imagine how a film director like Hong could go about his work without adequate vision.

Perhaps Hong's filmmaking can continue, despite this difficulty, since he does not necessarily rely on his eyesight to see the world. In fact, he will often focus on what is unseen, on the hidden side of reality. For Hong, his films are the result of arranging myriad life experiences in his mind. He notes: "I'm interested in the fragments of life. Writers might have great respect for sources of life and believe that the fragments of life drawn from these sources

Filmmaker Hong Sang-soo resists the mainstream influences in Korean cinema. He says: "I am often asked about the meaning of my films, but such questions can only be asked of those films that deliberately convey a certain message."

"On the Occasion of Remembering the Turning Gate" (2002) depicts a nameless actor wandering around in the countryside. Hong relies more on improvisation than scripts in shooting his films.

should maintain their original meaning. So they do not bother to arrange the fragments into different combinations. Or they think that the fragments themselves are meaningful. But I don't think that way. I think that if someone else arranged the incidents of life from a different perspective, a new interpretation could be possible. And that's how I believe things should be done."

He has never fully believed what he can see with his eyes, while striving to create something new by incorporating his own variations of what he might have seen. More often than not, the actors in his cast are similarly surprised by his unorthodox approach. Kim Young-ho, who acted in Kang's "Night and Day" (*Bamgwa nat*), recalled: "One day, I received the script and found out

that it included some of my own experiences. Incidents that I had mentioned to Hong, over drinks, became part of the story."

About this, Hong elaborated: "I use whatever I can from all manner of sources. From those sources, I obtain various ideas, details and fragments. It doesn't matter which sources they might have come from. I sometimes get ideas from totally unexpected sources." Hong's style is clearly distinctive from that of most film directors. Whereas most film directors are concerned with the creation of imagery, Hong focuses on an arrangement of countless fragments of life experiences in order to convey thoughts. These life experiences do not depend on what you can see, which might explain Hong's disregard for his failing eye-

Whereas most film directors are concerned with the creation of imagery, Hong focuses on an arrangement of countless fragments of life experiences in order to convey thoughts. These life experiences do not depend on what you can see, which might explain Hong's disregard for his failing eyesight.

sight.

His mother being a well-known film producer in the 1960s and 1970s, from early childhood Hong became familiar with the camera and film. As a result of this family environment, he does not think of a film as a commercial product for visual enjoyment; rather, it is a medium for personal expression of the inner self. Thus it seemed natural for Hong to enroll in the Department of Theater and Film of Chung-Ang University, as if setting out on a predetermined path. But he soon dropped out of school due to lack of interest in his courses and decided to study in the United States, where he learned all about film at the California College of the Arts and the School of the Art Institute of Chicago.

His 10-year-long study in the United States left an indelible imprint on his filmmaking career. He studied the basics of making films that differed from the mainstream style of entertainment movies, and became fascinated by the modern and post-modern experimental film genres. With the Korean film industry inhibited by heavy-handed censorship in the 1980s, innovative filmmaking was practically impossible except in adult films, such as "The Heyday of Young-ja" and "Madam Emma."

As such, it was hardly surprising that Hong's debut film, "The Day a Pig Fell into the Well" (1996), created a considerable stir among film critics in the country. Until that time, Korean movie makers had been satisfied with their portrayals of reality, which conformed to the prevailing atmosphere. But Hong broke new ground with his unconventional film. He remarked: "Andy Warhol showed scenes of the Empire State Building for eight hours, deriving new meanings from simple fragments. My films are similar to that. They present a new arrangement. I would say that with only a simple rearrangement, I pur-

sue something new." Then, he added: "There are films that consciously seek to convey a certain message. I am often asked about the meaning of my films, but such questions can only be asked of those films that deliberately convey a message." Rather than merely depicting reality, Hong seeks to reinterpret life experiences.

The film intelligentsia in Korea was highly impressed with Hong's post-modernist style, which featured processes of destruction and reconstruction. However, "The Day a Pig Fell into the Well" proved to be just a big splash in a small pond, leaving audiences in a state of bewilderment. Moviegoers were offended that its fragmentary scenes did not relate to a storyline or climactic finish. This lack of consumer appeal resulted in a box-office failure that left Hong with no resources for another project.

Still, Hong was undaunted. He said: "A film can be a medium to convey a meaning. And in making such a film, you focus on its effective expression. But I have a different attitude toward film. Everyone has his own inclination. However, movie audiences are so used to receiving a clear message that they reject a film if it is not easily understandable. There is pressure for a movie to deliver a certain meaning or message through a coherent process. That is always a burden for me."

Due to the commercial failure of his debut work, his second film, "The Power of Kangwon Province," was undertaken on a shoestring budget. The movie unfolds with seemingly random scenes of Gangwon-do Province. With no indications of a plot or direction, the film features a man and woman entangled in a messy love affair, who seem to wander aimlessly around the province. The film, however, provided a huge boost to Hong's career when it was invited to participate in the "*Un Certain Regard*" (A Certain Outlook) program at the Cannes Film Festival, marking the first time for a Korean filmmaker to be so honored. While the Japanese films of Akira Kurosawa and Kenji Mizoguchi had earned international recognition in the 1960s and 1970s, and the Taiwanese films of Hou Hsiao-hsien and Edward Yang were also highly regarded, Korean film remained on the margins. As such, the screening of Hong's film at Cannes represented a breakthrough for himself as well as the Korean film industry.

Hong's filmmaking style has also been evolving. Whereas "The Day a Pig Fell into the Well" and "The Power of Kangwon Province" reflected his efforts to adapt himself to the film environment in Korea, "Virgin Stripped Bare by Her Bachelors" enabled Hong to carve out his own niche in terms of creative style. During the shooting of this film, his eccentric ways were readily apparent. Moon Sung-geun, who has been cast in several of Hong's films, recalls: "Now, I am used to him, but at that time, it was quite strange. He doesn't explain anything and there is no script. Only when you see him in the morning, he hands you a script. Then you quickly look over the script and try to act it out. You cannot prepare at all."

Hong explains his unusual method: "I don't want the actors or actresses to prepare for their roles beforehand. If they do, their acting will be calculated. I give the actors as little information as possible because I want them to react more spontaneously to changing situations, rather than in a predetermined manner." Hong says that he gathers unfamiliar fragments within an overall framework to create new meaning. The cast's acting also provides certain fragments for his use. The fragments that he identifies in life involve the familiar as well as the unfamiliar. But simply combining refined fragments will not necessarily create something new.

The main character in Hong's films is always a version of himself. He strives to create new meanings out of unfamiliar fragments of life, while his inner self remains the original source of these meanings. Thereafter, the source is the inner self of the audience. Hong thus determines the principles and rules for his arrangement of fragments. He conceptualizes a film as having a spherical form that allows the viewer to select a perspective of his or her own.

He once described his approach by saying: "I make a film with a spherical form. It is different from a film that serves as a medium to convey a certain message or lesson, in which every element contributes toward its expression. Such a film, I would say, would have a triangular form, with a point at the top. I want my film to integrate numerous contradictions and interpretations so that viewers can adopt a perspective that contributes to their understanding. My film can be used as a means for people to understand themselves. One day, I received an e-mail. This person saw a film of mine and thought it was very sad. But a friend sitting beside her was highly amused. And someone else felt that my film belittled women. Actually, I want people to have different reactions."

Hong is attempting to do with his films what Picasso did with his paintings. Picasso sought to create three-dimensional images to depict all sides of an object, including its back that could otherwise not be seen. In this way, a viewer would not be restricted by a conventional perspective. Hong seeks to present an all-encompassing portrayal and his films are typically centered on a love story. Two people in love will tend to face each other, in which case it is not possible to see each other's back. But Hong considers it important to peer into the unseen for a broader understanding.

In recent years, Hong has struggled to maintain his artistic identity while searching for ways to overcome the barriers associated with the Korean film industry, which tended to resist his non-mainstream thinking. The high praises from film critics, which he garnered at the time of his debut, have since subsided. Nevertheless, there are others who have become ardent supporters of Hong over the years. This includes Goh Hyun-jung, a popular movie actress and unabashed fan of Hong, who says she would never hesitate to appear in his films. After taking a 10-year break from acting following her marriage, Goh was pleased to return to her acting career with a role in one of Hong's films.

Goh remarked: "Once I felt depressed, so I went to see a movie. All the other films were sold out, but there were still seats for a film directed by Hong. I enjoyed it. It was about a man and a woman, a love story, and it was entertaining, and at the same time made me think. So, I wanted to see all of his films. Whenever he makes a new film, I would be certain to see it." Her opinion has come to be shared by a growing number of moviegoers these days. She enjoyed "On the Occasion of Remembering the Turning Gate" (*Saenghwal-eui balgyeon*), which received tepid reviews from critics but was popular at the box office.

In 2008, Hong completed two films, a regular-length feature and a short film, which will be shown at this year's Jeonju International Film Festival. The feature film, "You Don't Even Know" (*Jal aljido mot hamyeonseo*), is about a film director and a film festival organizer. In an interview, Hong said: "Last year, I would often hear the expression: 'You don't even know.' Somehow this expression stuck in my mind, so I made a film out of it." His practice of gathering up the fragments of life, from here and there, is what his life is all about. Not only Goh Hyun-jung but other leading members of the cast, including Kim Tae-woo, Ha Jung-woo and Jung Yoo-mee, declined to accept their acting fees.

"You Don't Even Know" is likely yet another variation of the archetypical Hong cinema, with an absurd storyline similar to his previous works, in a kind of spherical form. Whether it would seem similar or different can vary according to the perspective of Hong or that of an individual viewer. Hong says: "I make a film, but I won't attach a particular ideology or message. That's the audience's part. People can enjoy or learn from what I do with my spherical-form film. Whatever they do doesn't actually matter. It doesn't matter if they don't like it or misunderstand its meaning. That's entirely up to them."

Shin Gi-joo Reporter, Premier Film   **Cine 21** Photographs

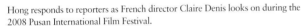

Hong responds to reporters as French director Claire Denis looks on during the 2008 Pusan International Film Festival.

Kim Ki-duk

Defiant Challenger to the Establishment

Whenever I see Kim Ki-duk, my first question is always the same: "What are you working on now?" But surprisingly enough, when I met him on a morning in June he said he was taking a break. Since his debut with "Crocodile" (*Ageo*) in 1996, he has completed 12 films in 10 years, always jumping from one project to another without interruption. But now this rebel, who seems intent on keeping viewers off balance with shock and outrage, lament and admiration, was just taking it easy.

Twelve films in 10 years is extraordinary to me, so I asked Kim about this: "It's not just the numbers, but when I reflect upon your recent films it seems that you are standing at an important turning point. So, what are your thoughts?" Suddenly, his face took on an odd expression, suggesting the confidence and conceit of someone who knows all the ordinary things of the world combined with his own far-sightedness and acknowledgement of reality. He responded: "Yes, 12 means I have made a dozen films. If each film is just one, I won't be able to make any more films. But if each film is not one but a dozen, I can go on making films."

At first, I could not understand his "dozen films"

notion, so I asked: "What do you mean that one is a dozen?" Then, with a playful expression as if to imply, "It's a sophisticated metaphor that may be difficult for you to understand," Kim explained: "What I mean is…" I got the idea. He had incorporated the esoteric philosophical concept of "the whole and the parts" into his own tangible, vivid and heartfelt experience as a director who had completed 12 films in 10 years, and sought to express this metaphorically. It seems that a conversation with Kim Ki-duk flows no more smoothly than any of his films when viewed for the first time. Above all, Kim is a serious intellectual, who is so enraged by all the evil and misfortune of the world around him that this resentment never allows him to relax.

As a film critic, I am an unabashed admirer of Kim Ki-duk and his work. I loved all of his films except for his second, "Wild Animals" (*Yasaeng dolmul boho guyeok*, 1997). His "Birdcage Inn" (*Paran daemun*, 1998) and "Spring, Summer, Fall, Winter and Spring" (2003) should be regarded as masterpieces not only in terms of Korean cinema but on a global level as well. But even more than the over-the-edge and provocative nature of his films, I greatly respect Kim's work ethic as he relentlessly makes

films with whatever resources that might be available.

Kim's filmmaking method can be described as follows. First, he reads and observes intently, then wanders about. If he has nothing in particular to do, he likes to read magazines in a library or roam around the city at random. While doing so, an idea for a film suddenly emerges. In the case of last year's "3-Iron" (*Binjip*), he was driving through a toll gate on an expressway when the image of a man entering a vacant house came to him. If an idea has potential, he thinks about developing it in one way or another. For "3-Iron," the image became an idea: "The man attaches an advertising flyer onto the door frame. If it is gone when he returns the next day, the house is occupied; if it is still there, the house must be vacant." This developed into a basic storyline for a film: "One day, a man entered a vacant house where an unfortunate woman was being kept captive." By then, the film was more than half done.

According to Kim: "In Korea, there are two kinds of film directors: bourgeois and proletarian. When a movie script is available, bourgeois directors start meeting with potential backers who, if they like the project, will agree to extend support provided star actors can be retained. Then the bourgeois directors start meeting with the star actors' managers to arrange the casting, and spend time making endless changes to the script to accommodate the schedule and personal whims of the lead actors and managers. In contrast, proletarian directors will start looking for filming sites as soon as they get an idea for a film. They then start making the film with whatever funds,

1 "Spring, Summer, Fall, Winter and Spring" (2003) questions the meaning of
   human life by comparing the life of a monk — from childhood, adolescence,
   adulthood and old age — with the four seasons of the year.
2 Kim Ki-duk achieved the remarkable distinction of winning the best director
   award in two out of three major international film festivals in 2004. "3-Iron"
   earned him the Award for Best Director at the Venice Film Festival.

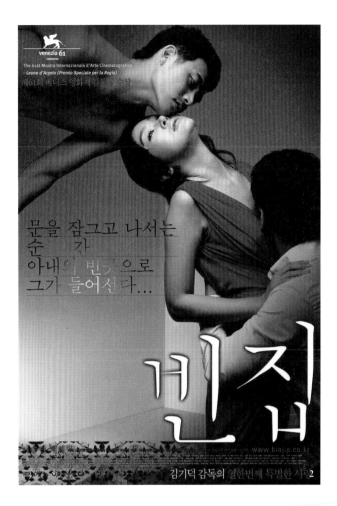

equipment and actors they can muster at the moment."

Having attended only elementary school and forced to work as an unskilled laborer, Kim is a true proletarian director. He was fortunate enough to complete elementary school. While Kim did not attend any of the universities that children of the bourgeoisie spend their youth competing for admission into, he came to see the world for what it really is. Instead of licking the rind of a watermelon and saying, "In English, this is called a watermelon," like some third-rate intellectual, he would smash a watermelon into bits and remark, "This is mostly water."

Kim knows well that human life is a miraculous sequence of one chance occurrence after another, which we only live once. He also knows that human wisdom is not acquired by getting down on your knees and praying, or by training the mind and learning about rationality, but by repeated attempts and failures to figure out the endless problems of existence, one at a time. The only way to attain wisdom is through trial and error experience. But for university-educated directors, it is all too easy to transpose life into an abstraction detached from reality. They come up with filmmaking goals from a rational perspective, and construct a theory and method to attain their objectives. But rationality is a particular thought process created by modern Western philosophers. Rationality is not encoded in human genes. Furthermore, rationality and the mind are not actual realities but merely chemical reactions among nerve cells of the brain.

Instead of seeking to construct the world and relying on rationality for ideas, Kim simply jumps up and starts doing whatever. By trying and failing, he learns by doing, from one personal experience after another. This self-taught individual who never studied film, has learned by making films, all the while steadily honing his unique film style. Evidence of Kim's success includes receiving Best Director awards from Europe's most prestigious film festivals as well as breaking new ground in the distribution of independent films in the U.S. market. Kim is a truly remarkable success story, showing how it is possible for a self-made man to become a world-class film director. But instead of appreciating his impressive success, Korea's aspiring film directors continue to view Kim with skepticism.

Kim does not hesitate to take issue with film critics. Indeed, he seems intent on making films that challenge the prevailing values and systems of the Korean film industry as well as the mainstream standards advocated by film critics. Prior to his recent rise to fame, in response to the mass media's disparagement of his films, he submitted a letter of protest to a newspaper under the headline "Crocodile Tears." He refuses to grant interviews with film magazines that are critical of his films and despises critics who give him no respect. From this year, he has decided not to submit his films for consideration for Korean film awards and pledged to decline any such recognition. For the release of his latest film, "The Bow" (*Hwal*), in Korea, he did not offer a press preview and provided only a single photograph to the media. Kim thus declared that film critics and journalists should go to the theater and buy

1 Kim receives the Award for Best Director at the 61st Venice Film Festival in September 2004.
2 Kim's 12th film, "The Bow" was invited for viewing at the "*Un Certain Regard*" (A Certain Outlook) section of the 2005 Cannes Film Festival.

It seems that a conversation with Kim Ki-duk flows no more smoothly than any of his films when viewed for the first time. Above all, Kim is a serious intellectual, who is so enraged by all the evil and misfortune of the world around him that this resentment never allows him to relax.

a ticket to see the film. Naturally, with many critics and journalists refusing to view his film as paying customers, it was seen by only some 1,500 viewers and ended up a box-office failure. So, why does Kim choose to be so defiant?

Although he is now recognized as a world-renowned director, Kim remains an outsider in Korea. In particular, this is because his films feature men who ruthlessly abuse and exploit women, or people living in poverty who are unable to look beyond their unfortunate plight, while only bickering and turning against each other. As a result, Kim has been condemned as ignorant, uncultured, and a perpetrator of gender discrimination, while being relegated to the periphery of cinema circles.

But since seeing his first film "Crocodile," I have felt that Kim was a man of deep compassion. And it is because of this compassion that he despairs at the injustice and misfortune of the real world and seeks to express this lament through extreme outrage. Really evil people do not bother to insult others but merely sneer. Kim explains it this way: "For me, the task of making a film is a process of attempting to convert a world of misunderstanding into one of understanding." I believe this is not merely brilliant word play but a vivid portrayal of his true conviction. Unlike too many intellectuals, Kim is not a narcissist

of rationality and ethical niceties. After scraping through elementary school, he endured a hard life as a factory worker, and even as a youth he rebelled and acquired a worldly self-confidence as well as an understanding of how things work that intellectuals might learn only after long immersion in countless philosophy books.

Kim has not yet decided on his next film. He is taking a short break for now, allowing his defiance to subside. Meanwhile, various film ideas have come into his mind, but nothing that inspires him. The film that he really wants to make is the story about the Korean troops who were unwittingly thrust into a massacre during the Gwangju Democratic Uprising in May 1980. Perhaps the film should be entitled "Poclain." Poclain is a brand name used by a French maker of construction equipment for a backhoe. Kim bought a backhoe a while ago that was used for building his studio near Yangpyeong. While riding home with him in a jeep, I asked him: "Couldn't you have just rented a Poclain?" The answer was typical of Kim. "No, it's so much fun operating a Poclain. Don't you know it's better to own something than to borrow it?"

Kang Han-sup Professor of Film, Seoul Institute of the Arts
Choi Hang-young Photographer